November 8/2010

Deb, I want to participating and anniw... the 2011 Supply management Strategic Planning session.

I hope you find the reading insightful and helpful in your leadership journey

I am really looking forward to working with you to execute and deliver the 2011 plan, and to see the Construction Group excel in 2011!

Thanks

Dalw.

What Twenty-Two of the World's Greatest Leaders and Thinkers Say about *Mojo*

"Those of us who have been lucky enough to spend time in a classroom with Marshall Goldsmith know what a positive influence his teaching can have. In *Mojo,* Marshall shares his scholarship more broadly and teaches us all how to turn inertia in our professional or personal lives into meaning and happiness. There is no more important lesson in business or in life!"

—Tom Glocer, CEO, Thomson Reuters

"As soon as I started reading this book, I felt my *Mojo* rising. The next best thing to being coached by Marshall is reading his books. His writing always gets me revved up and focused on getting the most meaning and happiness out of my day. This book can elevate any reader's game."

—Mark Tercek, CEO, Nature Conservancy;
former Managing Partner, Goldman Sachs

"Marshall Goldsmith is one of a kind: a unique and brilliant combination of getting inside our minds about those problems which keep us awake at night—and not only clarifying, but actually solving them! Lively and engaging. A damn good read, which every leader will not only enjoy, but profit from."

—Warren Bennis, bestselling author, Distinguished Professor at
USC, and world authority on leadership

"Marshall's books are very much like Marshall—insightful, direct, focused, wise, clear, somewhat provocative, positive, lively, and energetic. For those who have not worked with Marshall and experienced these qualities, his latest book, *Mojo,* is a great substitute. *Mojo* is like him—a little crazy, yet very helpful!"

—Jonathan Klein, CEO, Getty Images; *American Photo*'s
"Most Important Person in Photography"

"Marshall has a gift for identifying the essential ingredients of success—for individuals and organizations. The insights in *Mojo* are certain to help people at all stages of their career tap their full potential and live more fulfilling lives. Another great book, Marshall!"

—John Hammergren, CEO, McKesson Corporation;
winner, Warren Bennis Award for Leadership

"Mojo is elusive, hard to define, at least as old as homo sapiens . . . and worth its weight in gold. This thoughtful and thought-provoking book should be read by anyone who has tasted *Mojo* and wants more."

—Kevin Kelly, CEO, Heidrick and Struggles,
global search and advisory firm

"Marshall helps leaders, aspiring leaders, and anyone who wants to enrich their personal and professional lives focus on actions that provide both meaning and happiness. *Mojo* is a great reminder that we're most likely to enjoy success in our careers and lives when we regularly take the time to be honest with ourselves."

—Chris Kubasik, President, Lockheed Martin;
Chairman, Sandia Corporation

"Marshall provides an array of case studies where he combines business challenges around navigating in the 'new normal' with real tools—tools for yourself and tools for you to help others that you care about. Thanks to Marshall for providing another wonderful read, with both short term and longer term ideas for personal growth."

—Teresa Ressel, CEO, UBS Securities LLC;
former Chief Financial Officer, U.S. Treasury

"Marshall clearly articulates the payoff—for your company, your family, your community, and yourself—of having more meaning and happiness in your life. And he provides a compelling and clear road map for getting you there."

—Greg Brown, President and CEO, Motorola

"One more great book by Marshall! With his typical depth, simplicity, and clarity, he helps me understand, accept, and improve my *Mojo* with lasting positive impact!"

—Fabrizio Parini, CEO, Lindt (Italy); former CEO,
Ghirardelli Chocolate

"Marshall Goldsmith is tops at the hardest part of the alphabet—ABC, adult behavior change. We give him high marks!"

—Charles Butt, CEO, H-E-B,
one of America's 20 largest private companies

"Marshall is a master at helping people gain self awareness. *Mojo* provides great food for the soul. Reading this book makes me feel like I am listening to Marshall!"

—Liz Smith, CEO, OSI Restaurant Partners,
a world leader in casual dining

"Again, Marshall has his finger on the pulse of the worker and the workplace. This clear, insightful, and wise book helps employees find their *Mojo*. It helps them move beyond commitment and find ways to truly contribute in their professional and personal lives. The greatest power in the workplace is the workforce and Marshall has figured out how to unlock that potential."

—David Ulrich, professor, University of Michigan;
co-author of *The Why of Work*

"Emerson once wrote, 'What lies behind us and what lies before us are small matters compared to what lies within us.' *Mojo* focuses on that which lies within us, what we do with it, and how others perceive it resonating from us. A wonderful read!"

—Alan Hassenfeld, former Chairman,
Executive Committee, Hasbro

"Looking for that special sauce that produces extraordinary success? *Mojo* is it. Once again, Marshall's wisdom and generosity light up the pages."
　　—Keith Ferrazzi, bestselling author of *Never Eat Alone*
　　　　and *Who's Got Your Back*

"Marshall provides sound, practical advice and illustrates it through real world examples. He provides a road map to increasing your personal happiness and outlines steps to get back into the groove. A great plane read!"
　　—George Borst, President and CEO, Toyota Financial Services

"A great strategy book for life! Innovative ideas to help you find happiness and meaning."
　　—Vijay Govindarajan, professor, Tuck School of Business;
　　　　Chief Innovation Consultant, GE; world authority on strategy

"*Mojo* is a rich collection of insights into the human experience and practical techniques for improving the quality of our lives. Marshall's a master teacher and communicator, and his self-disclosing stories and style make this a delightful as well as powerful read. It's a superb primer for getting along in uncertain times, with much more fun and meaning along the way."
　　—David Allen, bestselling author of
　　　　Getting Things Done and *Making It All Work*

"Put your *Mojo* in gear! Marshall again inspires us to knock down the obstacles, overcome the barriers, and take charge of ourselves."
　　—Joe Scarlett, CEO (retired), Tractor Supply Company;
　　　　founder, Scarlett Leadership Institute

"Marshall Goldsmith does it again! A must-read book! Strikes a deep chord in each of us—about what really matters in our lives and work. At no time in history have more people and organizations needed to get their *Mojo* back. This book tells you how!"
　　—Mark Thompson, bestselling author of *Success Built to Last;*
　　　　Forbes magazine's Venture Investor with the Midas Touch

"We all want to get our *Mojo* working. Marshall Goldsmith helps us to understand *what* our mojo is and *how* to get it working . . . to our advantage and for our self-worth."

    —Jim Lawrence, CFO, Unilever

"Marshall Goldsmith is a master at making us think more deeply about ourselves and the world we work in. *Mojo* is a grabber—uniquely provocative—and moves the reader to act. Quite a gift!"

    —Jon Katzenbach, bestselling author of *The Wisdom of Teams*;
      Senior Partner, Booz & Company

Professional Recognition for Marshall Goldsmith

The Institute for Management Studies—Lifetime achievement award (one of only two winners in the past twenty-five years).

American Management Association—Top fifty thinkers who have influenced the field of management over the past eighty years.

National Academy of Human Resources—Fellow of the Academy (America's top HR award).

The (London) Times, Forbes—Top fifteen most influential business thinkers in the world (a biannual study involving over 3,500 respondents and an expert panel).

BusinessWeek—One of the most influential practitioners in the history of leadership development.

The Wall Street Journal—Top ten executive educators.

Economist (UK)—Most credible thought leaders in the new era of business.

Leadership Excellence— One of the top five thought leaders in management and leadership.

Economic Times (India)—Five leading raj gurus of America.

Fast Company—America's preeminent executive coach.

MOJO

**ALSO BY
MARSHALL GOLDSMITH**

What Got You Here Won't Get You There

Mojo

HOW TO GET IT,

HOW TO KEEP IT,

HOW TO GET IT BACK

IF YOU LOSE IT

Marshall Goldsmith

with Mark Reiter

HYPERION

NEW YORK

Library of Congress Cataloging-in-Publication Data has been applied for.

ISBN: 978-1-4013-2327-1

Hyperion books are available for special promotions and premiums. For details contact the HarperCollins Special Markets Department in the New York office at 212-207-7528, fax 212-207-7222, or email spsales@harpercollins.com.

Book design by Karen Minster

FIRST EDITION

10   9   8   7   6   5   4   3   2   1

THIS LABEL APPLIES TO TEXT STOCK

We try to produce the most beautiful books possible, and we are also extremely concerned about the impact of our manufacturing process on the forests of the world and the environment as a whole. Accordingly, we've made sure that all of the paper we use has been certified as coming from forests that are managed to insure the protection of the people and wildlife dependent upon them.

Mojo is dedicated to my friend, co-writer,

and agent Mark Reiter. Is my life better

because I have met Mark Reiter?

In more ways than I can even count!

Thank you, Mark!

Contents

SECTION IV

Connecting Inside to Outside

Acknowledgments

Mojo would not have been possible without the help and support of many wonderful people:

- My wife, Lyda, son, Bryan, and daughter, Kelly, who manage to love me in spite of my crazy writing and traveling schedule.

- My wonderful coaching and leadership development clients—who have taught me far more than I have ever taught them. I feel so privileged to work with many of the most successful and inspirational leaders in the world. As good as they are—they are still striving to get better!

- The wonderful teachers who have helped me: David Allen, Richard Beckhard, Warren Bennis, Niko Canner, Fred Case, Peter Drucker, Keith Ferrazzi, Vijay Govindarajan, Phil Harkins, Sally Helgesen, Paul Hersey, Frances Hesselbein, Jon Katzenbach, Bev Kaye, Gifford Pinchot, CK Prahalad, Mark Thompson, Dave Ulrich, and John Ying.

- My friend and editor, Sarah McArthur, who endlessly reviews everything I write and provides valuable assistance.

- Alliant International University, Marshall Goldsmith School of Management—and the Global Leadership Development Center team: Chris Coffey, Ron Curtis, Jim Goodrich, Maya Hu-Chan, Bill Hawkins, Tom Heinselman, Carlos Marin, Howard Morgan, Jim Moore, Linda Sharkey, and Frank Wagner.

- Jackson & Coker—leaders in physician recruitment, whose research is helping to shape my teaching about *Mojo*.

- Extended DISC—especially Markku Kauppinen, who is conducting great research on identity and *Mojo*.

- Hyperion—This is my second book with the wonderful folks at Hyperion. It started with two men named Will: Will Schwalbe, who endorsed the idea instantaneously but left to find his Mojo as an Internet entrepreneur; and Will Balliett, who was instrumental in shaping its contents and reminding me to get words on paper. Eventually, it landed in the calm, capable hands of Brendan Duffy. The support of Ellen Archer and Kristin Kiser cannot be underestimated.

- The Center for Leadership Studies—which has taught me as well as supported my work.

- Dartmouth's Tuck School, Michigan's Ross School, the Scarlett Leadership Institute, HarvardBusiness.org, BusinessWeek.com, HuffingtonPost.com, Dale Carnegie, Linkage, the Conference Board, AMA, ASTD, HRPS, SHRM, ChartHouse, Talent Management, and the Institute for Management Studies—which have helped my work reach millions of leaders.

- Heidrick & Struggles—which has helped me shape my thinking about leadership development.

- The inspirational men and women in the military and human services organizations who serve every day—not for money or glory, but to help others.

- Buddha—who knew more about human behavior two and a half centuries ago than anyone I have ever met in my lifetime.

- And finally, you, my readers. Your support means more to me than you will ever know. If you ever want to talk, please send me a note at Marshall@MarshallGoldsmith.com. I can't get back to you instantly, but I almost always get back eventually.

Despite all of the contributions of these wonderful folks, I am sure that this book, like everything else I have done, has a few dumb remarks. For these, I take responsibility and apologize to you. As Buddha said so well—please use what works for you and just "let go" of the rest.

"I am awake."
—BUDDHA

You and Your Mojo

CHAPTER 1

Mojo, You, and Me

A few years ago I attended a girls' high school basketball game with my friend Mel and his family. Mel's daughter Chrissy was her team's starting point guard. It was the league championship and we were all hoping for the best.

But in the first half, Chrissy and her teammates could do nothing right. As they headed toward the locker room at halftime, they were down by seventeen points, their shoulders were stooped, and I could see a couple teammates arguing with each other. The coach was swinging his clipboard like a traffic cop, hurrying the girls as if he were afraid things might get worse if they didn't get off the court as quickly as possible. The game was so lopsided that I was dreading the second half. I could see Mel thinking the same thing: *Please Lord, no more of this.*

But we reminded ourselves that anything's possible, that Chrissy's team could claw back and at least make the game interesting. And that's precisely what happened.

Chrissy and her teammates opened the half with a couple of three-point shots and a steal that led to an easy layup. In what seemed the blink of an eye, a daunting lead of seventeen points had been trimmed to a more manageable nine points. And Chrissy's team didn't let up. They continued to chip away until they trailed by only three. The opposing team's coach finally called a time-out and everyone on our side stood up to applaud our team's thrilling comeback.

Mel turned to me and said, "We're gonna win this game." And at that moment, I knew exactly what he meant.

The evidence was on the court. The entire tone of the game had changed. While in the first half Chrissy's team had been confused, now they were prowling the court with a renewed sense of urgency and a little more swagger. You could see it in their eyes. Each player was thinking, *Give me the ball. I can do it.* You could see the change come over the other team as well. While in the first half they were operating in a smooth, wordless flow as they built up their enormous lead, now they were tense, bickering with each other, whining about the referees, and turning more frequently to the bench, where their coach was gesturing wildly and trying to settle them down.

Chrissy's team did, in fact, go on to win the game. Who can say why a confused, dispirited team emerged from halftime with a different attitude? Perhaps they found a communal purpose in the embarrassment of being down by seventeen points. Perhaps their coach gave them a new game plan. Or maybe they won the game simply because of the boost of confidence that came with the good fortune of starting the second half with a string of small successes that produced eight unanswered points. Maybe all of these factors combined to lift the team's spirit from negative to positive.

What I remember most vividly about that game was that moment when Mel turned to me and we both *knew* that Chrissy's team would do just fine. We all felt it, and our natural response was to stand up and cheer.

That moment is the condition I call Mojo. It is the moment when we do something that's purposeful, powerful, and positive, *and* the rest of the world recognizes it. This book is about that moment—how we can create it in our lives, how we maintain it, and how we recapture it when we need it again.

To some degree, we're all familiar with Mojo. If you've ever given a speech—and done it well—you know the feeling. I realize that public speaking is one of people's greatest fears; many people would rather crawl through a snake-filled swamp than talk in front of a crowd. But if you're a remotely successful adult, chances are you've had to speak in public at some point. It might be a sales pitch to a customer. It might be an internal presentation where you defend your work to your bosses and peers. It might be a eulogy at a loved one's funeral, or a toast at your daughter's wedding. Whatever the occasion, if you've done it well—if the audience hangs on every word, nods in agreement, laughs at your jokes, and applauds at the end—you've created the same feeling that was spreading across Chrissy's high school gymnasium. You're firing on all cylinders *and* everyone in the room senses it. That is the essence of Mojo.

The word "mojo" originally referred to a folk belief in the supernatural powers of a voodoo charm, often in the form of a piece of cloth or a small pouch. (That's what Muddy Waters was referring to in his song "Got My Mojo Working.") That quasi-superstitious meaning persists for some people. I know one entrepreneur who doesn't go to work without playing five hands of gin rummy with his wife. "If I win," he told me, "I've got my Mojo. If she wins, I don't sign any contracts that day."

Over time the word has evolved to describe a sense of positive spirit and direction, especially in the shifting tides of sports, business, and politics. It could be a politician in a tight election coming off a couple of weeks of successful error-free campaigning that results in a favorable jump in the polls; suddenly the pundits anoint him as the candidate in the race with Mojo. It could be a colleague who pulls off a string of moneymaking deals; suddenly everyone has to admit—some grudgingly—that she is "on a roll," that she's found her Mojo.

To other people, Mojo is a more elusive sense of personal advancement through the world. You're moving forward, making progress, achieving goals, clearing hurdles, passing the competition—and doing so with increasing ease. What you are doing matters and you enjoy doing it. Sports people call this being "in the zone." Others describe it under the umbrella term "flow."

My definition of Mojo spins off from the great value I attach to finding happiness and meaning in life.

Mojo plays a vital role in our pursuit of happiness and meaning because it is about achieving two simple goals: loving what you do and showing it. These goals govern my operational definition:

Mojo is that positive spirit toward what we are doing now that starts from the inside and radiates to the outside.

Our Mojo is apparent when the positive feelings toward what we are doing come from inside us and are evident for others to see. In other words, there's no gap between the positive way we perceive ourselves—what we are doing—and how we are perceived by others.

Four vital ingredients need to be combined in order for *you* to have great Mojo.

The first is your *identity*. Who do *you* think you are? This question is more subtle than it sounds. It's amazing to me how often I ask people this question and their first response is, "Well, I think I'm perceived as some-one who . . ." I ask them to stop immediately, saying, "I didn't ask you to analyze how you think *other* people see you. I want to know who *you* think you are. Taking everyone else in the world out of the equation, in-cluding the opinions of your spouse, your family, and your closest friends, how do you perceive yourself?" What follows is often a long period of si-lence as they struggle to get their self-image into focus. After people think for a while, I can generally extract a straight answer. Without a firm han-dle on our identity, we may never be able to understand why we gain—or lose—our Mojo.

The second element is *achievement*. What have you done lately? These are the accomplishments that have meaning and impact. If you're a sales-person, this might be landing a big account. If you're a creative type, it could be coming up with a breakthrough idea. But this too is a more subtle question than it sounds—because we often underrate or overrate our achievements based on how easy or hard they were to pull off.

For example, one of the most senior human resources executives I know told me she could pinpoint the exact moment her career took off—although she thought nothing of it at the time. She was the assistant to her company's CEO. One day she heard him complaining about the com-pany's tracking system for expenses. That night she wrote a memo to the CEO on how she would streamline the system. It didn't require much effort or brainpower on her part; as someone who had been filling out the CEO's travel and entertainment reports for years, she had a very good sense of the reimbursement system already in place. But the memo impressed her boss, who almost immediately moved her into the human resources de-partment, where she could shake things up with her ideas. In her manager's eyes, she clearly demonstrated insight, initiative, and executive ability—and her memo became the moment that jump-started her career from as-sistant to where she is today, overseeing hundreds of employees.

That's just one example of what might be defined as a "small" achieve-ment, but was really a big one.

We will look at achievements from two perspectives: (1) What we bring to the task, and (2) What the task gives to us. Until we can honestly put a value on what we've accomplished lately, we may not be able to cre-ate or regain our Mojo.

The third element is *reputation*. Who do other people think you are? What do other people think you've done lately? Unlike the questions about identity and achievement, there's no subtlety here. While identity and achievement are definitions that you develop for yourself, your reputation is a scoreboard kept by others. It's your coworkers, customers, friends (and sometimes strangers who've never met you) grabbing the right to grade your performance—and report their opinions to the rest of the world. Although you can't take total control of your reputation, there's a lot you can do to maintain or improve it, which can in turn have an enormous impact on your Mojo.

The fourth element to building Mojo is *acceptance*. What can you change, and what is beyond your control? On the surface, acceptance—that is, being realistic about what we can and cannot change in our lives and accommodating ourselves to those facts—should be the easiest thing to do. It's certainly easier than creating an identity from scratch or rebuilding a reputation. After all, how hard is it to resign yourself to the reality of a situation? You assess it, take a deep breath (perhaps releasing a tiny sigh of regret), and accept it. And yet acceptance is often one of our greatest challenges. Rather than accept that their manager has authority over their work, some employees constantly fight with their bosses (a strategy that rarely ends well). Rather than deal with the disappointment of getting passed over for a promotion, they'll whine that "it's not fair" to anyone who'll listen (a strategy that rarely enhances their image among their peers). Rather than take a business setback in stride, they'll hunt for scapegoats, laying blame on everyone but themselves (a strategy that rarely teaches them how to avoid future setbacks). When Mojo fades, the initial cause is often failure to accept what is—and get on with life.

By understanding the impact and interaction of identity, achievement, reputation, and acceptance, we can begin to alter our own Mojo—both at work and at home.

Mojo appears in our lives in various guises. Some people have it for almost everything they do, no matter how unpleasant the activity may seem to others. Some have it, lose it, and can't seem to get it back. Some lose it and recover it. And then there are those who have it in some parts of their lives but not in others.

Which of the following examples sounds familiar to you?

Case 1. Aside from my parents and family members, Dennis Mudd was the first "great person" in my life. Not "great" in the sense of a Winston Churchill or Buddha—who altered the lives of people they never met—but great nonetheless because, in his modest way, he had a lasting positive impact on the people he did meet.

When I was fourteen years old and living in Kentucky, the roof on our home started to leak badly. So my father hired Dennis Mudd to put on a new roof. To save money, I was dragooned into assisting him. To this day, putting on a roof in the middle of a Kentucky summer is the hardest physical labor I've ever done. But it was eye-opening because I got to work every day with Mr. Mudd—a man with naturally abundant Mojo. I was amazed at the care Mr. Mudd put into the laying of the shingles. Nothing was left to chance. Everything had to be perfect. Mr. Mudd was patient with me as I made mistakes. If a tile was loose or out of line, he would help me rip it up and show me how to lay it down correctly. In hindsight, it's quite possible that my assistance actually slowed Mr. Mudd down, but he never mentioned it. After a while, I became "infected" by Mr. Mudd's joyful spirit toward the job of roofing in the hot summer sun. My attitude changed from "grudging willingness" to "pride in a job well done." Each morning, I woke up looking forward to working on the roof.

When the project was finally over, Dennis Mudd presented my dad with an invoice and said, "Bill, take your time and inspect our work. If this roof meets your standards, pay me. If not, there is no charge." Mr. Mudd wasn't kidding, even though not getting paid would have been a serious financial hit for him and his family.

Dad examined the roof, complimented us on a job well done, and paid Dennis Mudd—who then paid me.*

---

* This roofing experience, no doubt, made an impression on me, because when I became an executive coach I patterned my compensation after Dennis Mudd's. I only get paid if my clients get better. "Better" means my clients achieve positive, measurable change in behavior, as judged not by themselves or by me, but by their key stakeholders—namely, their clients' managers, colleagues, and direct reports. This process takes twelve to eighteen months and involves an average of sixteen stakeholders. Whenever I'm asked how I came up with this "pay for results" idea, I always credit Dennis Mudd, who was my boss forty-seven years ago. Although I am proud of what I do, I still believe that Dennis Mudd demonstrated more "class" than I ever have. I'm fortunate in that if I didn't get paid, my life would not be too adversely affected. Dennis Mudd needed that money much more than I do, yet he was still willing to risk it to do what was right for his clients. (continued on p. 9)

That pay-me-what-you-think-it's-worth gesture was not a stunt. It was an expression of Mr. Mudd's identity. I realize now, five decades later, that his pride in the quality of his work made this a low-risk proposition. He was confident other people would see the quality—and pay him what he deserved. Not only did he harbor an internal positive spirit toward what he was doing, but also it showed on the outside in a way that other people could not miss. That is Mojo in its purest form.

Case 2. Chuck is a "former" TV executive who was once one of the top leaders in his industry. He was responsible for breakthrough ideas that you can still see evidence of on the air—and he still knows as much about his field as anyone in the business. He has been a "former" TV executive for five years—in other words, that's how long he's been out of work. And it's not that he hasn't been aggressively pursuing another job: With his contacts and credibility, he can pick up the phone and talk to any powerful decision-maker he wants. That's an enviable position to be in, and though he hasn't abused it, he's discussed his situation with virtually everyone in a position to help him.

Over the years he's picked up the occasional consulting assignment, hoping that it might turn into a permanent job, but nothing has materialized. He's now fifty-five years old. The longer he's out of work, the less likely it is that he will get work. If you haven't worked in your field for half a decade, there comes a point when you can't call yourself a "TV executive" anymore.

Through severance packages and sound investments, Chuck has saved enough money to provide for his family. But the situation is taking a toll on his psyche and confidence. Lately, he's begun worrying about what kind of role model he has been for his children. Do they see him as a

---

In 2006, after I mentioned Dennis Mudd in a magazine, a native of my hometown, Tom Masterson (who was later recognized as Small Business Person of the Year in Kentucky by President Obama), sent me this note: "In his later years, Dennis Mudd drove the bus that took me to high school. It was a 37-mile drive. He always tried to get us there 15 minutes before school started. During this time I would stay on the bus and talk with him. We talked about everything in life and he had a tremendous influence on me. I cannot tell you what a thrill it was to read this article and think about him again."

Dennis Mudd was able to change one life while building a roof and another life while driving a school bus. And I know that he influenced many others. He had the kind of positive spirit toward what he was doing that I have seldom seen matched by highly paid professionals doing so-called "dream jobs."

success, or as someone who's been hanging around the house for five years? It also pains him to see leadership positions at TV networks, cable channels, and production companies now being occupied by some of the people he once hired and trained. He's begun talking more and more about the glory days when he was on top. He prefers reminiscing about the past to dealing with his future.

Friends have told him that he should start up his own production company. When he was on top, he was one of the best "idea men" in the business. He could still use that talent to develop projects that he could pitch to his deep list of contacts. With that initiative, he'd be back in the game, dealing with potential customers as an equal rather than scratching at their doors for favors. But because of either inertia or fear, Chuck can't do it. He doesn't *want* to work for himself. He wants to work for a big organization. That's all he's ever done. That's all he knows. He wants to dial back his life to the way it was before he lost his job.

Chuck is counting on a stroke of luck. But he's not doing what's required to create that luck. His identity is wrapped up in a past that grows more distant and foggy by the day. His past achievements—some five years old, some much older—are no longer relevant. His reputation— what he thinks of himself—is no longer in sync with what others think.

But Chuck's biggest error is one of acceptance. He's still hoping to find a job that replicates his last one. The only problem—which he refuses to acknowledge—is *that job no longer exists for him.* Until he accepts that, Chuck's Mojo will never come back.

Case 3. The date: July 7, 1956. The place: the Newport Jazz Festival in Newport, Rhode Island.* It's Saturday night. Duke Ellington and his band are scheduled to perform. The fifty-seven-year-old Ellington has had a rough go of it in recent years. In the 1930s and '40s, playing hits like "Take the A Train" and "Mood Indigo," he led the greatest big band ever. But changing musical tastes and the cost of touring with sixteen musicians have put a dent in Ellington's success. The summer before, in 1955, the Ellington orchestra was reduced to accompanying ice skaters at a rink

---

* I know, I know. The mere mention of jazz makes some readers' brains shut down. But bear with me. It won't kill you, and there's a great ending!

on Long Island. When your name implies royalty, it doesn't get lower than that.

Ellington is anxious to do well at Newport. He has composed a new piece, "The Newport Festival Suite," for the occasion. But the night does not begin auspiciously. Four of his band members don't show up, and festival producer George Wein asks Ellington to open the evening with "The Star Spangled Banner." After two more tunes, as people in the audience are restlessly milling about under a humid summer sky, Ellington is waved off the stage to make way for other performers. Ellington is indignant. "What are we, the animal act? The acrobats?" he asks.

He has to wait three hours before returning to the stage. It's near midnight and at least a third of the audience has gone home. But Ellington is still angry and determined to put on a great show. He is down—but not out. He has played the new composition and two more numbers, when a light rain begins, sending people to the exits.

To get them back, Ellington calls for one of his standbys, the up-tempo "Diminuendo and Crescendo in Blue," written in 1937. It's a two-part piece which Ellington usually connects with one of his piano solos. But tonight he lets tenor saxophonist Paul Gonsalves do the honors. Gonsalves launches into a furious solo and people return to their seats. Ellington senses the audience's change in mood and urges Gonsalves to keep it up; he won't let him stop. Two minutes into the solo, the normally sedate crowd, which was heading for home a few minutes earlier, begins to roar with approval. An attractive blonde in a strapless summer dress gets up near the stage and starts dancing. More people begin to dance. Onstage, Ellington and the band are shouting words of encouragement to Gonsalves. The crowd is in such a frenzy that producer Wein frantically signals to Ellington to cut the number short. He's afraid of a riot. "Don't be rude to the artists," Ellington shouts back, wagging his finger. Gonsalves solos for nearly seven minutes. As the tune ends, the crowd rushes the stage. Wein again pleads with Ellington to leave the stage for safety's sake. Ellington refuses and continues through four encores.

The next day the band's performance is a front-page international sensation. "Ellington Is Back!" shout the headlines. A few weeks later *Time* magazine puts Ellington on the cover. A recording of the Newport appearance is rushed out and sells more than a million copies, becoming the most successful release of Ellington's career. Ellington is reborn. He never works a skating rink again, and goes on to produce an astonishing body of new work in the later years of his career. When he turns seventy, his birthday party is held at the White House.

It's tempting to treat this as a tale of redemptive luck: a great performer on the downswing revives his career through a heroic last-stand miracle of timing and circumstance. But if we dig a little deeper we see the mechanics of Mojo at work. Even as his popularity ebbed, Duke Ellington never abandoned his love of performing. He still maintained his orchestra and continued to tour nonstop, covering any losses out of his own pocket. Being a working musician is who he was. His reputation had taken a hit as musical tastes changed, but his identity (working musician) and achievements (classic tunes) were intact and undisputed. He still felt a positive spirit about what he was doing. Newport let him radiate that spirit to the outside world. At Newport, the crowd finally saw what Ellington knew all along. At Newport the world heard Duke Ellington the way he heard himself.

Case 4. Janet isn't a good strategic leader; she is a *great* strategic leader. She is regarded as the best pure businessperson in her company, even better than the CEO. She can combine strategic brilliance with a knack for execution—a rare skill. She hires great people and coaches them along the way. Nothing matters more to her than developing—and nurturing—her team. People love working for her. She consistently produces fantastic results, not only from quarter to quarter, but with innovations that will pay off in the future.

But something goes seriously wrong for Janet when she steps outside her "circle of trust" and has to deal with people at corporate headquarters. The same instinct that leads her to nurture and protect her team turns into an unfortunate defensiveness when she finds herself among other division heads. Despite her track record, Janet feels like she has to prove herself to her peers. She vigorously competes with them for resources and support, often too vigorously, which her peers see as an unattractive "us versus them" attitude. In meetings, she has to "win" every debate, which Janet sees as appropriate competitiveness but her peers regard as alienating and uncooperative. They wonder why she can't acknowledge the validity of someone else's point of view once in a while and work to help everyone win.

Janet has a severe case of split Mojo—high in one area of her work, low in another. (In this regard, she is not unlike many other high-functioning people. Computer programmers and engineers are classic examples: high Mojo when they're engaged in creative problem-solving, low Mojo when they have to deliver documentation.) When she's working with her team, Janet's Mojo is "off the charts." When she's working with her peers, it's at rock bottom. The positive spirit she radiates among her people turns negative among her colleagues at headquarters—and it shows.

This wouldn't be an issue if Janet could be cordoned off and left alone to run her team. But her CEO regards her as star material, a potential successor to her boss (and perhaps in ten years or so, a potential CEO). Leading a major product group, she makes decisions that impact all of her company's departments, but Janet possesses Mojo in only *part* of her job, and no matter how gifted she is, she cannot ignore her peers or play the "Lone Ranger" role forever. Her next position on the corporate ladder would put her in charge of many of the executives she's currently alienating. The CEO believes that promoting Janet now could send a lot of her peers walking out the door.

Janet's challenge is to take her obvious business and people skills and apply them to all of her key stakeholders, including the peers who can make or break her future. She has the potential to run the entire organization some day, but not until she learns to nurture her colleagues as well as she does her direct reports. If she doesn't do that, the status quo will stop rewarding her. Eventually, her negative spirit will consume her identity and reputation. One of her peers will become her boss—and she'll discover that when you pursue a double life of high and low Mojo, it's the low Mojo that may result in the most lasting impression.

For much of my career as an executive coach, I've defined my mission as helping my clients achieve positive change in their interpersonal behavior. That mission hasn't changed—I still want to help people develop better relationships—but for reasons that will become manifestly obvious, in *Mojo* I will focus on our *internal* workings—and our personal definitions of meaning and happiness.

When I wrote *What Got You Here Won't Get You There* in 2007, my inspiration was Peter Drucker's quote "Half the leaders that I have met don't need to learn what to do. They need to learn what to stop." I went on to identify twenty-one behaviors that were holding back otherwise successful people in their careers—annoying transactional habits such as *winning too much, making destructive comments,* or *punishing the messenger.* In that book I focused on helping people transform their behavior and their image.

In this book I'll be focused on what people can *start* doing in order to achieve more meaning and happiness in their lives. That's the payoff of having Mojo. More meaning. More happiness. It's not just for organizational leaders; it's for all of us, and it applies to all aspects of our lives because, as our research (to be shared later) clearly documents, people with high Mojo at work tend to have high Mojo at home.

My goal is to provide an extended answer to the most frequently asked question I hear in my work: "What is the one quality that differentiates truly successful people from everyone else?"

My short answer is always the same: Truly successful people spend a large part of their lives engaging in activities that simultaneously provide meaning and happiness. In the terms of this book, *truly successful people have Mojo.*

Then I add: The only person who can define meaning and happiness for you is *you!*

That's what this book is about.

Look around you. It's now the second decade of the twenty-first century, and circumstances have changed. Whether it's something immediate and temporary, like the shrinking price of your home, or watching your 401K turn into a 201K, or the shaky job security of your friends and neighbors, or something larger and more lasting, like the vulnerability of once-mighty businesses—newspapers and magazines—shutting down daily or financial giants going *poof* overnight. The challenges in our society bleed into our personal lives. Professionals are working longer hours and feeling more pressure than ever before. With new technology that keeps us connected 24/7, the boundaries between professional and personal, work and home blur. The quest for meaning and happiness becomes more challenging, and yet more important than ever.

These are confusing times indeed, heaping damage not only on the Mojo of people who are out of work or in financial jeopardy but also on other people who are seemingly living the American dream.

My client Jim was a mega-successful entrepreneur who founded a company and sold it for more money than he could have imagined. He and his family moved to a beautiful home in the country. He seemed to have it all, but within an alarmingly short period of time all of this Mojo vanished. He quickly tired of playing bad golf with old men at the country club and eating the same chicken salad sandwich at the same table every day while discussing gallbladder surgery—and who they "used to be." He "coasted" like this for nearly two years—which he now describes as the worst years of his life. His growing dissatisfaction began to alienate his wife and kids and annoy everyone around him. He felt that his life had become meaningless. He said he felt "worse than a bum." While a poor bum might be cursed with an addiction and mental problems, in addition to poverty, Jim chided himself for "having it all" and doing nothing with what he had.

He eventually recaptured his Mojo by focusing on philanthropic activities that engaged his problem-solving skills and allowed him to make a contribution. He re-injected into his life the same kind of meaning and happiness that he had felt while building a business. It felt familiar *and* different, but it was all good.

If smart people like entrepreneurs who've hit the jackpot can't get a fix on their Mojo, imagine how tough it is for people without such comfortable cushions to fall back on.

People like Jim and Mel and Chuck and Janet are among the dozens of people you'll meet here. You'll recognize some of them because they're no different than your colleagues and neighbors. In some cases you may think you're looking at yourself in a mirror. None of us has all the answers. All of us falter and lose our Mojo at some point along the way.

The good news is that nearly all of the challenges we'll deal with here have simple—although not easy—solutions (there's a difference between simple and easy). You'll find these solutions in the book's third section, which I call "Your Mojo Tool Kit." Some of these "tools" are obvious, some are counterintuitive, but they are all within your reach. They are to a businessperson's Mojo what a three-pointer is to a basketball team's. They are difference makers.

But first, let's turn the page to determine how much Mojo you have—or have lost.

CHAPTER 2

Measuring Your Mojo

How much Mojo do you have? How do you know if you have any at all? How can you measure your Mojo? Before you start measuring your Mojo, let's focus on understanding what Mojo is—and isn't—and what its absence looks like.

You know that definition of Mojo I tossed out so casually in the previous chapter? The one that said "Mojo is that positive spirit toward what we are doing now that starts on the inside and radiates to the outside"? I didn't come up with it blithely or quickly. It took me some time.

For a while I thought of Mojo as another word for momentum—merely a function of *direction* (how do I become who I want to be, starting from where I am now?) and *speed* (how quickly can I make that happen?).

But then I realized that this definition assumed that to have Mojo people had to be striving to be different or better than they were now. Not true. There are plenty of people who demonstrate great Mojo and are not trying to change—they are finding happiness and meaning in their lives *right now.* How do we account for *that*?

I also realized that there are people who by all external measures—money, respect, power, status—are "winning." They are outpacing their peers and competition quite handily, thank you. And yet inside they derive little satisfaction or meaning from their job or achievements. I suspect that we all know someone like this: seemingly set for life on the outside yet dissatisfied on the inside. How do we account for *that*?

That's when I realized that Mojo is not merely about the rush we feel when we're on a winning streak. It's not *only* about the direction we're heading in, nor is it about the pace of change we're creating around us. Mojo is an expression of the harmony—or lack of harmony—between what we feel inside about whatever we are doing and what we show on the outside.

That's the thinking behind my operational definition of Mojo. I stress the phrase *operational definition,* which may not be familiar to you. It's a concept I learned from my mentor Dr. Paul Hersey, one of the pioneers in the field of organizational behavior. When Dr. Hersey discussed broad terms such as "leadership" or "management" in his classes, he would always begin with an operational definition of each. Paul knew that such open-ended terms were ripe for semantic debate and that different people ascribed different meanings to them. Without clear, operational definitions, he might be talking about one thing, while his students might be hearing something else. He made no claims that his definitions were *better* than anyone else's. He merely noted that, for the purposes of his class, these definitions were what he meant. I was amazed at how much time and energy Dr. Hersey saved by never arguing about the "right" or "best" definition. That's one reason Paul was such a great teacher: When he spoke, his students always knew what he was talking about.

So please imprint the following operational definition for Mojo in your mind.

Mojo
is that positive spirit
toward what we are doing
now
that starts from the inside
and radiates to the outside.

I've divided the sentence into parts, as if it were poetry, because each part deserves some special attention.

Positive spirit is unambiguous. It's a feeling of optimism and satisfaction. It conveys both happiness and meaning.

Toward what we are doing focuses us on the fact that we're dealing with an activity or a task—as opposed to a state of mind or a situation. For example, when we assess our Mojo at work, we're not assessing the size of our office, the proximity of our parking space, or the digits on our paycheck. Those are conditions, not actions. We're assessing the various layers of our engagement in the job we are doing. We can assess Mojo at home as well as work in considering activities that involve our friends and family members.

Now's meaning is obvious, though its importance cannot be overstated. When we are measuring our Mojo, we do so in the immediate present, not in the recent past or vague future. Our Mojo in the past is over because, for better or worse, we've changed since then. It's like reading week-old news. Our future Mojo is impossible to measure because it hasn't happened yet. It's a fantasy, still unreal. Happiness and meaning can't be experienced next week, next month, or next year. They can only be experienced now. That's why the most successful professionals are always "on" when they're engaged in their craft. They're not distracted or saving themselves for later. In their professions, it is always now for them. They love *what* they are doing *when* they are doing it. They are finding happiness and meaning in the *present*.

That starts from the inside is my reminder that measuring Mojo is an exercise in self-assessment. There are no "right" or "wrong" answers. No external instructors handing out grades. Only *you* know what you're feeling. Only you can score yourself. It also reflects a lesson I've learned from my executive coaching: *Nobody ever gets better because of me.* I can provide help and point the way, but the improvement from my clients is self-generated; it has to come from inside them—not inside me.*

And radiates to the outside is my nod to the cause-and-effect dynamic between what we feel inside, how much of it we show, and how it is perceived by others. People who love what they're doing but somehow never show it are doomed to be misunderstood. Their Mojo and their careers do not reach their full potential. Likewise, people who hate what they're doing but manage to paint a convincing picture of positive spirit on the outside are phonies—and their inauthentic act usually catches up with them.

---

* In my career, the coaching client who took the least amount of my time demonstrated the most improvement. Whereas the coaching client who took the most amount of my time did not improve at all. If my involvement was the key variable for achieving lasting positive change, more interaction with me would have led to more improvement. But it just doesn't work that way.

No single segment of this definition of Mojo is more important than the others. Remove one and the concept crumbles. But the unifying element is *radiates to the outside*. To everyone who has to deal with you, this is the part that makes all the difference.

Not long ago I put a dent in the rear fender of my car. It was one of those accidents that happen at two miles an hour less than a hundred feet from home. But still, the damage was done: a spherical indentation the size and depth of a basketball. I took the car to a dealership where I was told that because the fender was made of a plastic composite, not metal, it couldn't be hammered back into shape. I'd need a new fender and rear quarter-panel assemblage for $1,800. Ouch. I thought I could get a better price at a nearby body shop, but I got the same response for the same price. Ouch again. A neighbor, seeing the dent, suggested I try a new body shop several miles away. I drove over without an appointment, and I was greeted by the owner, a young man in his mid-twenties. He assessed the damage and said, "It's plastic all right, but sometimes you can apply heat and the material bounces back to its original shape. Why don't you go inside, have a cup of coffee, and I'll try heating it up. If it works, we'll be done in half an hour. If not, we'll talk about other options."

I had my coffee in the waiting area and after thirty minutes asked the young lady at the counter, "How's my car?"

"He's just finished with it—it's all fixed," she said. "The charge is $63.75, including tax."

I asked her if she was sure, handed her my credit card, and walked outside to my car, still staring incredulously at my receipt.

The young man was standing by my car, beaming and pointing to the fender where the dent had vanished and the paint had been beautifully touched up. All completed in thirty minutes for less than $100.

I thanked him, we shook hands, and as I walked around to get in the car, he said, "Isn't it nice to meet a repairman who is trying to *save* you money?"

That young man is a paragon of Mojo. That he was willing to experiment on his own time with my fender, in order to save me time and money, proved that he had a positive spirit inside. But the kicker was seeing him stand proudly by his finished handiwork. It was his unequivocal way of radiating that positive spirit so that the rest of the world could see it. A man who takes more delight in doing his job well, even at the expense of some easy profit, is rich in Mojo. He will never starve.

My young mechanic made this look easy, but sometimes no matter how positive we feel about what we're doing, we fail at showing it on the outside. We are so focused on completing our task that we assume people can read what's in our hearts and minds. We think our good intentions should be obvious. They can't possibly be misconstrued.

This happened to an executive named Derek whom I met a few years ago. He was a new plant manager who had been "flown in" to upgrade the performance of a failing plant. If he didn't turn things around, the plant would be closed and all the employees would be laid off. Derek's bosses had low expectations of success, but they assured Derek that his job was safe no matter the outcome. "Just give it your best shot," they told him. In his six months on the job, Derek grew to love the people in the small town that surrounded the plant. He was impressed by their friendliness to an outsider. He also knew how much these jobs meant to the town's future. If he failed, families would suffer. He was working eighty hours a week to save the plant and feeling a lot of pressure.

I met Derek when he participated in a company-wide leadership development program that I was conducting. As part of the program, Derek received confidential 360-degree feedback from his direct reports and co-workers. When I reviewed the results with him, he was stunned. His scores on "treating people with respect" were among the lowest in the company.

"I can't believe people say I don't respect them," he ranted. "I am busting my butt to help them, and this is the thanks I get."

When he calmed down, he and I went over the written comments, which clarified the issue. Derek was trying so hard to save the plant that he didn't realize how he was coming across to people. While he thought he was demanding Herculean efforts from everyone—including himself—in a team effort to save their jobs, the others saw him as continually stressed out, angry, judgmental, and dissatisfied. He yelled at subordinates over innocent mistakes. He was always "barking out" orders and not listening to the people he professed to love. As he reflected on his daily behavior, Derek realized that there was a clear disconnect between the respect he *felt* for the people around him and the respect he *showed* in his day-to-day interactions.

"It's like a parent who wants his child to succeed so much that he ends up badgering and bullying the child," Derek said. "I was beating them up in order to save them. That didn't make sense."

Derek took his feedback to heart and committed to change. He let everyone know that he was aware of the incongruity between what he was feeling on the inside and showing on the outside. He asked for a second chance.

When I caught up with Derek a year later, his scores on "treating people with respect" had improved dramatically. He was now seen as a motivational rather than a de-motivational force at the plant. He was able to buy time for the plant with his bosses and still stay focused on turning things around. He continued fighting a hard battle, but he was seen as a "happy warrior" rather than an "angry warrior." On a personal level, he was less stressed out and more at peace with himself.

All of this is what makes the last part of our definition so important. If the activity involves other human beings, we cannot assume that the spirit we're feeling on the inside is the spirit we're showing on the outside. We sometimes have to work at making sure our positive emotions are communicated, and this may take more effort than the activity itself.

That Negative Spirit Called Nojo

Paul Hersey also taught me that in defining a term, it's often useful to think about its opposite. It wasn't much of a struggle to come up with a word that describes the opposite of Mojo. It was literally on the tip of my tongue when I thought about people who had *that negative spirit toward what they are doing now that starts from the inside and radiates to the outside.* They have Nojo! We all know people like this: bored and frustrated in their jobs, confused about the dark tunnel their career has fallen into— and not shy about sharing their bitterness with the rest of the world. Even the sound of Nojo describes them perfectly—no joy!

The contrasts between Mojo and Nojo are sufficiently stark that I jotted them down in a cheat sheet:

MOJO	NOJO
Take responsibility	Play the victim
Move forward	March in place
Run the extra mile	Satisfied with the bare minimum
Love doing it	Feel obligated to do it
Appreciate opportunities	Tolerate requirements
Make the best of it	Endure it
Inspirational	Painful to be around
Grateful	Resentful
Curious	Uninterested
Caring	Indifferent
Zest for life	Zombie-like
Awake	Asleep

Nowhere is the difference between Mojo and Nojo more evident to me than in the service economy, especially when I'm confronted by two employees doing exactly the same job at the same time. Take air travel, for example. I've been traveling 185 days a year for three decades. On American Airlines alone I just passed the dubious milestone of ten million frequent flyer miles. I have interacted with thousands of flight attendants. Most are dedicated, professional, and geared to providing excellent service. They demonstrate Mojo. A few are grumpy and act like they would rather be anywhere else than on the plane with me. They demonstrate Nojo. Both the Mojo and Nojo flight attendants are doing exactly the same activity at the same time for the same company at the same salary for the same customers, yet the message that each is sending to the world about his or her experience couldn't be more different.

A restaurant, with its waiters and waitresses, is an arena for Mojo gazing that's even more instructive than observing flight attendants. Restaurants occupy both ends of the economic scale—from expensive gilded palaces of fine dining to cheap roadside diners—so you see all types of people. As a patron, you always have some personal interaction with a waiter (sometimes too little, sometimes too much, and sometimes just enough). And at the end you give the waiter a performance review in the form of a tip.

It's pretty easy to tell who wants to be waiting tables and who'd rather be doing something else. In France, waiting on tables is generally seen as an honorable career, not a fallback position of last resort. In the United States, people may become waiters and waitresses because it's the only job available or because it's a relatively flexible job that they can do while they pursue something else. In cultural capitals like New York or Los Angeles, it often seems that half the waiters are would-be actors, painters, or writers. There's nothing wrong with that. People have to make a living while they perfect their craft or audition for parts or write that first novel.

What I find interesting about waiters, at least in terms of Mojo, is the wide variety of attitudes that people bring to a narrowly defined job that ends with a monetary tip. Since waiting tables is one of the most direct play-for-pay jobs in our economy you'd think that waiters would reliably take people's orders, deliver the food, pay attention without hovering, be engaging without intruding, and correct mistakes promptly—in short, focus on what they have to do in order to earn the biggest tip. After all, that's why they're waiting on tables.

The best ones appreciate the process. They appreciate the work itself. So no matter how they feel about their circumstances, they radiate a positive spirit (high Mojo). Their customers usually take note of this positive spirit when calculating the tip. The waiter's Mojo literally translates into cash.

The worst ones make it a point of honor to let you know that they find the job demeaning (low Mojo), that they are really more interesting in their *other* life (with more Mojo). If they let that attitude ruin their customers' dining experience, their negative behavior translates into a smaller tip.

Also on the low Mojo end of the scale are the waiters who treat the job as menial work. It's not that they have another life that represents the *real* them. They simply need the job and don't have any other alternative. They're not that intrigued by the subtleties of waiting on people and they're not getting any personal satisfaction out of it.

Finally, there are the career waiters. You're more likely to find them in fancy big-city restaurants (where the checks and tips are big). They are waiters by choice, not by accident or desperation. There's a professional snap to how they do their job, and they never hint that they would rather be doing something else. They are committed to doing the task well and they are capable of mining personal satisfaction from it. If they have a bad day, they don't take it out on their customers. They get paid well and they deserve it!

My friend John Baldoni was recently conducting a leadership seminar. John used the "Mojo" and "Nojo" framework to describe various levels of employee engagement. One of the participants said, "I'll bet everyone in this room can make a list of the employees in our company who are role models of Nojo!" He then added, "And we all wish that they would 'Gojo'!"

The Mojo Scorecard

In thinking about flight attendants and waiters, it's clear that the job itself does not define Mojo. After all, the great and not-so-great flight attendants are doing identical jobs. Mojo has to be about something else, I concluded. But how do you measure it?

That's when it hit me. We all have two forms of Mojo in our lives: Professional Mojo, which is a measure of the skills and attitudes we bring to any activity, and Personal Mojo, which is measured by the benefits that a particular activity gives back to us.

Within this framework, it was easy to construct a simple test that we can use to measure our Mojo when preparing for any specific activity. Five qualities that we need to bring to an activity in order to do it well are: motivation, knowledge, ability, confidence, and authenticity. Likewise, five benefits we may receive from the activity after doing a job well are: happiness, reward, meaning, learning, and gratitude.

Here's the test. Think of a typical day in your life. Pick one of your more important activities. Rate yourself on each of the ten questions on a scale of 1 to 10, with 10 being the highest. A perfect Mojo score would be 100.*

---

* In the unlikely event that you score 100 on the Mojo Test for every element of your life every day, stop reading this book and give it to someone who *really* needs it.

MEASURING YOUR MOJO

PROFESSIONAL MOJO: What I Bring to This Activity

1. **Motivation:** You want to do a great job in this activity. (If you are just "going through the motions" when you are engaged in this activity, your score would be low.)

2. **Knowledge:** You understand what to do and how to do it. (If you are unclear on processes or priorities, your score would be low.)

3. **Ability:** You have the skills needed to do the task well. (If this activity does not fit your talents or competencies, your score would be low.)

4. **Confidence:** You are sure of yourself when performing this activity. (If you feel unsure or insecure, your score would be low.)

5. **Authenticity:** You are genuine in your level of enthusiasm for engaging in this activity. (If you are "faking it" or being insincere, your score would be low.)

PERSONAL MOJO: What This Activity Brings to Me

6. **Happiness:** Being engaged in this activity makes you happy. (If it is not stimulating, creates misery, or is otherwise non-joyful, your score would be low.)

7. **Reward:** This activity provides material or emotional rewards that are important to you. (If the activity is unrewarding or if the rewards do not matter to you, your score would be low.)

8. **Meaning:** The results of this activity are meaningful for you. (If you do not feel a sense of fulfillment or that you're contributing to a greater good, then your score would be low.)

9. **Learning:** This activity helps you to learn and grow. (If you feel that you are just "treading water" and not learning, your score would be low.)

10. Gratitude: Overall, you feel grateful for being able to do this activity and believe that it is a great use of your time. (If it seems like a poor use of your time or you regret doing it, your score would be low.)

That's it. A fairly simple test: ten questions that you can answer in a short period of time.

One caveat: Although it's a simple test, it's not necessarily easy—largely because it's a self-assessment test, with no right or wrong answers. You determine your own score. But that virtue is precisely what makes it hard. Many successful people have a tendency to overestimate their strengths and underestimate their weaknesses. We often think we're smarter, better-looking, and more accomplished than the facts may bear out. Keep that in mind as you assess your Mojo. If, for example, you award yourself a 10 for knowledge or ability in a specific activity, that 10 may be a red flag that you're letting ego trump the truth. Most of us have room for improvement, especially when it comes to knowledge and ability. Even Tiger Woods might hesitate giving himself a 10 in ability for certain aspects of being a golfer. So step back and ask yourself if your colleagues would award you the same score. If you still believe it, so be it. Remember, no one else is seeing the test results. They're for your eyes only. There's no good reason to lie to yourself. This is for you!

This is not a one-time test. Because it takes so little time, it's something you can—and should—do throughout the day as you participate in different activities. (In fact, you can download a Mojo Scorecard at MojoTheBook.com.) The Mojo Scorecard is no different than a golfer's scorecard. In golf you write down your score against par after every hole, then add up your strokes at the end of the round to gauge how you did. The card lets you see where you did well during the round and where you faltered. You can do the same with the Mojo Scorecard. After every discrete event or project during the day—whether it's a two-hour lunch meeting, or a five-minute phone call with a customer, or a half-hour session to return e-mails, or the end of a long trip—jot down your scores in all ten areas. When you finish your next activity, score yourself again. Do this until the end of your working day. Then add up the scores, divided by the number of activities, to determine your average Mojo score for one full day at work.

Do this for a few days and patterns will emerge. You'll see areas of strong Mojo and areas of weakness. You'll also discover which recurring activities provide you with the most satisfaction. For example, one media executive who filled out the Scorecard told me that his highest Mojo—by far—occurred at midday, right before he returned to the office from lunch. He said, "Basically, the one part of my job that really pleases me is lunch."

"Is it the food or the company?" I asked.

"Neither," he said. "It's the situation itself. Lunch for me is either an information-gathering activity or a selling opportunity. It's generally with people in the business I know well and like. If they're strangers whom I'm meeting for the first time, I'm not going to have lunch with them. That's too risky. What if we don't get along, or there's no chemistry, or no areas of mutual interest? That's a long, exhausting lunch—for both of us. So lunch is not only with someone I like, but someone who's in my field. We trade information and industry insights. We share ideas and try to solve each other's problems. That's a really fun and satisfying conversation for me, especially if I get to use my expertise to advise someone. Or vice versa: My lunch partner shares something new with me that I can use to my advantage. That's a win-win. One of us gets the satisfaction of helping a friend, the other gets the help. Even better, there's always a moment at lunch when I slip in a pitch for my services. I love the process of selling, of trying to get people to buy my product line. That's the one time in my day when I know I'm in full flower—using my best talents for the maximum reward."

Given that explanation, the executive's Mojo Scorecard would show 8s, 9s, and 10s at lunch. That's an important chunk of self-knowledge that he had never considered until he reviewed his Scorecard. (Lesson learned for him: Make more of his day just like lunch.)

Another lesson emerges when we score ourselves. We learn that all of us *have more than one role during the day*. I'm sure that if we all subdivided our daily activity into discrete tasks, we'd see that we function in several roles, not just one. For example, a middle-management executive at different points in a day may be leading people, or attending a meeting, or putting out fires, or asking people for money, or filling out reports and shuffling paper. That's five distinct roles—as a boss, an employee, a crisis

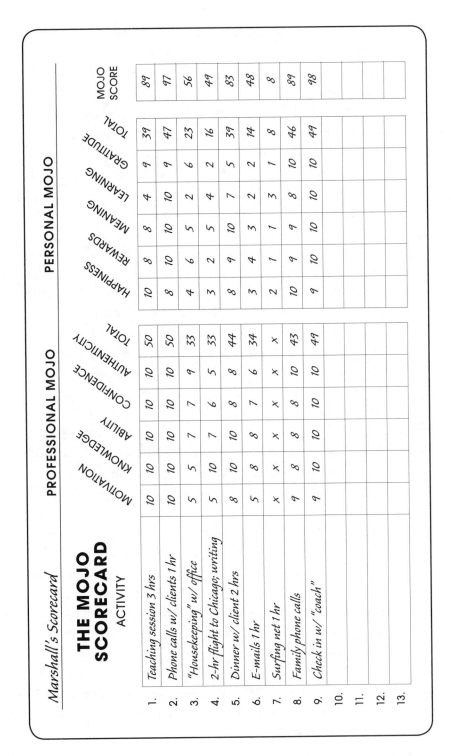

THE MOJO SCORECARD

Marshall's Scorecard

| ACTIVITY | PROFESSIONAL MOJO | | | | | | PERSONAL MOJO | | | | | | MOJO SCORE |
---	MOTIVATION	KNOWLEDGE	ABILITY	CONFIDENCE	AUTHENTICITY	TOTAL	HAPPINESS	REWARDS	MEANING	LEARNING	GRATITUDE	TOTAL	
1. Teaching session 3 hrs	10	10	10	10	10	50	10	8	8	4	9	39	89
2. Phone calls w/ clients 1 hr	10	10	10	10	10	50	8	10	10	10	9	47	97
3. "Housekeeping" w/ office	5	5	7	7	9	33	4	6	5	2	6	23	56
4. 2-hr flight to Chicago; writing	5	10	7	6	5	33	3	2	5	4	2	16	49
5. Dinner w/ client 2 hrs	8	10	10	8	8	44	8	9	10	7	5	39	83
6. E-mails 1 hr	5	8	8	7	6	34	3	4	3	2	2	14	48
7. Surfing net 1 hr	x	x	x	x	x	x	2	1	1	3	1	8	8
8. Family phone calls	9	8	8	8	10	43	10	9	9	8	10	46	89
9. Check in w/ "coach"	9	10	10	10	10	49	9	10	10	10	10	49	98
10.													
11.													
12.													
13.													

manager, a salesperson, and a clerk—for which he or she may have widely divergent Mojo scores.

Many of us engage in serious roles that exist beyond the borders of our day job, such as being a volunteer, or a parent, or a Little League coach. If an activity matters to you, whether it's your primary breadwinning activity or something you do "after hours," let's get it on your Mojo Scorecard. It cries out for assessment.

Our Mojo at home is just as important, if not more important, than our Mojo at work!

Here's my Scorecard for a typical day in my professional life:

TASK 1: The first discrete measurable "event" of my day was a three-hour teaching session, from 8 A.M. to 11 A.M., that I conducted for a group of thirty human resource professionals in Stamford, Connecticut. I love teaching. It is probably what I do best. I didn't learn as much from teaching on this day as I learned from some of the other elements of my job (hence the lower score on learning), but I found this teaching experience to be both meaningful and rewarding. I gave a lot to "it" and it gave a lot to "me."

TASK 2: From 11:30 A.M. to 12:30 P.M. I made scheduled phone calls to clients. I love interacting with my clients—and this was one of those times when everything seemed to go just right.

TASK 3: From 12:30 to 1 P.M. I engaged in "housekeeping" chores via the phone with my San Diego office, while riding to the airport for a flight to Chicago. This is something that I may need to do, but don't love doing. Upon reflection, what I learned from my score may be that I don't have to do all of this myself. (A benefit of the Mojo Scorecard—it causes us to question the elements of our lives that are just not working.)

TASK 4: Devoted two-hour flight to Chicago to writing this book. On this day, writing was very tough for me. I got distracted—and didn't do a good job.

TASK 5: Had early dinner with a coaching client, the chief operating officer of a family-owned manufacturing company. This session went well, but by the end of the dinner I was tired—and not sure I should have scheduled this meeting at this hour.

TASK 6: Originally scheduled two hours for writing time on this book. But then spent first hour of the time answering e-mails. This is an activity that I felt I needed to do, but didn't love doing. My scores show it.

TASK 7: Spent second hour of planned "writing time" surfing the Internet. This was not really a "professional" activity—so I didn't score the "professional Mojo" boxes. Upon reflection, it wasn't even personally rewarding; it was largely a waste of my time. My learning point—beware of mindless net surfing!

TASK 8: Phone calls to my family. This was one of the most meaningful and rewarding parts of this day.

TASK 9: Regular 10 P.M. telephone check-in with my "coach" to review checklist of my goals. On this day, my session with my coach was both personally and professionally rewarding.

While I am often described as an executive coach, it is clear from my Mojo scorecard that my life is filled with a variety of very different activities.

When looking at the scorecard, I noticed that I experienced high levels of Mojo when I was teaching or coaching. I also loved learning and communicating with my family. My job as a writer is very important to me, but much more challenging. I tend to be extroverted and love interacting with people. It is tough for me to spend the "alone time" needed to be a great writer. Over the years, I have improved—but still believe that I have a lot of work to do in order to write at a level of quality that my readers deserve.

When I was dealing with the basic chores of maintaining my business life, my Mojo scores dropped significantly. Like most humans, I just wasted part of the day. On this day, "surfing the net" didn't bring me any professional benefit—and wasn't even that much fun. It was just a waste of my time!

As you can see by my review of the day, we can learn a lot about ourselves from our Mojo Scorecard. We can learn where we may need to spend more time—and where we should try to find others to help us. We can learn where we may need to "adjust our attitude" in situations where we may have to do something that we don't normally enjoy.

I'm not trying to paint complexity into my work life. In many ways, I lead a simple life. I teach leaders in group sizes that run from several hundred to just one person. I talk on the phone a lot. I sit at my laptop and write. And I spend an inordinate amount of time in airport lounges and on planes, getting from one place to another. Different tasks, different roles. But each of those activities represents a different facet, a different part of my life. And I need to account for that when I ask myself, "How am I doing?"

In reviewing the complexity of my life, I'm not that much different than most successful multitasking businesspeople in the twenty-first century:

- The hard-charging executive, who's still single and spends much of his free time taking care of his aging parents, has two major roles, one professional, the other personal: businessman and son.

- The creative director at an advertising agency who wears more hats than she can count: She writes, she illustrates, she pitches for new accounts, she manages people, she nurtures talent, and she is often the high-profile public face of the entire agency. That's at least six roles, perhaps more.

- The founder of a small business, who can do (and has done) every job in the company, from the shop floor to the back office to the showroom and the front office, and could conceivably lay claim to so many roles that we would simply give up and lump them all into one macro-job that we'd label *entrepreneur* or *owner*.

Everyone's day requires different skills and produces different levels of Mojo. That's why the first step in establishing or recapturing your Mojo is a test to determine what you bring to each activity in your day—and what each activity brings to you. Without the test, you might never pin-point all the daily tasks that gobble up your time, or realize whether these tasks actually matter to you. Also, you might never appreciate that each activity, in some form or another, represents a different facet of you, a different part of your life. Once you add up the numbers on your Scorecard, you might finally be forced to pause and ask yourself, "Is this really what I should be doing?"

CHAPTER 3

The Mojo Paradox

When I work with successful people to help them figure out "what really matters" in their lives, five key variables emerge (not in order of importance):

- Health
- Wealth
- Relationships
- Happiness
- Meaning

While my previous books have focused primarily on building positive relationships, Mojo will focus on two other ingredients for a truly successful life: happiness and meaning.

As much as we all claim to want happiness and meaning in our lives (very few people say that they want to live miserable, empty lives), there's a paradoxical catch that thwarts us at every turn. I call it the Mojo Paradox and I want you to burn it into your memory:

Our default response in life is not to experience happiness.

Our default response in life is not to experience meaning.

Our default response in life is to experience inertia.

In other words, our most common everyday process—the thing we do more often than anything else—is *continue to do what we're already doing.*

If you've ever come to the end of a TV show and then passively continued watching the *next* show on the same channel, you know the power of inertia. You only have to press a button on the remote (an expenditure of less than one calorie of energy) to change the channel. Yet many of us cannot do that. Quite often, inertia is so powerful that we can't even hit the remote to turn the TV off! We continue doing what we're doing even when we no longer want to do it.

Inertia is the reason I can say the following with absolute certainty about your immediate future: The most reliable predictor of what you will be doing five minutes from now is *what you are doing now*. If you're reading now, you'll probably be reading five minutes from now. The same is true for almost any other daily activity. If you are drinking or exercising or shopping or surfing the Internet now, you will probably be drinking or exercising or shopping or surfing the Internet five minutes from now. Take a moment to let that sink in and weigh the statement against your own life.

We carry that bad mood from our work to our home. We carry that bad mood from our home to our work. I'm not saying that inertia is a foolproof predictor (we obviously switch from one activity to another), but it is an incredibly reliable short-term predictor.

Once you appreciate the Mojo Paradox, you become aware of its paralyzing effect on every aspect of your life, not just the mindless routines of eating or watching TV, but also things that really matter—such as the level of happiness and meaning in your life—and you become more thoughtful about turning things around.

How do we break the cycle of inertia? It's not a matter of exerting heroic willpower. All that's required is the use of a simple discipline.

Before I get to that, let me give you some backstory. About twenty years ago I was preparing a leadership development session for a Fortune 100 company, when one of the company's senior managers asked me a perfectly plausible question: "Does anyone who goes to these leadership sessions ever really change?"

My candid answer was "I don't know." Although I had been conducting these sessions for years with dozens of companies, I had never followed up with my clients to see if, later on, they actually took the sessions to heart, did as I'd instructed, and became more effective leaders. So I began going back to many of my clients and assembled data that answered the question, "Does anyone ever really change?" Our original follow-up study included 86,000 respondents. Our database has grown to more than 250,000 respondents. My conclusion is now unequivocal. *Very few people achieve positive, losting change without ongoing follow-up.* Unless they know at the end of the day (or week or month) that someone is going to measure if they're doing what they promised to do, most people fall prey to inertia. They continue doing what they *were* doing. They don't change their behavior, and as a result, they don't become more effective. On the other hand, if they know someone, like their coach, their coworkers, or their manager, is watching—in the form of paying attention to them, or caring about them, or evaluating them with follow-up questions—they're more likely to change.* The key is measurement and follow-up, in all their myriad forms.

Now, what if we didn't have to rely on an "outside agent" such as a manager or executive coach to do follow-up that initiated real positive change? What if we could be that "change agent" for ourselves? What if there was a regimen where we could ask the follow-up questions and provide the answers to ourselves?

That's what I'm proposing here as the solution to the Mojo Paradox. It comes in the form of an experiment I want you to try.

As you go through your day, I want you to evaluate every activity on a 1 to 10 scale (with 10 being the highest score) on two simple questions:

#1. How much long-term benefit or meaning
    did I experience from this activity?
#2. How much short-term satisfaction or happiness
    did I experience in this activity?

Simply record the activities that make up your day, both at work and at home, and then evaluate each activity by applying these two questions.

There is no "right" answer. There is no acceptable range of scoring. No one else can answer the questions for you. It's *your* experience of

---

* I published the research on the original 86,000 respondents with my partner Howard Morgan in "Leadership Is a Contact Sport: The 'Follow Up Factor' in Management," *Strategy+Business*, Fall 2004, pp. 71–79.

happiness and meaning. Give it your best shot. Don't "think it to death." Just take a couple of seconds and record your scores. At the end of the day you will have a chart that tracks your experience of happiness and meaning.

If you do this, you may end up with much more than a score.

It is my firm belief that if you journey through life knowing that all of your activities will be evaluated on these two simple questions, you will tend to experience more happiness and meaning in each activity and, in the aggregate, you will have a happier and more meaningful life.

The simple knowledge that you're going to evaluate any activity will alter your experience of that activity. It makes you more mindful and awake. The dynamic is no different than if you knew that you would be observed and graded by your manager on a task. Chances are that you would perform the task better than if you knew there would be no evaluation. That's human nature. We've obeyed it since we were little kids in school, goofing off when the teacher left the room and instantly resuming our best behavior when the teacher returned. We're more alert to how we behave, perform, and appear to others when we know someone is judging us. The only difference in this experiment is that you are the one asking the questions and doing the evaluation.

I'm convinced that this ritual of self-directed follow-up works because I've seen it work both in my coaching practice and in my own life. The mere act of evaluating an activity forces you to break the pattern of inertia enveloping that activity.

For example, let's imagine that you're curious about a subject—say, vacations in the south of France—so you fire up your laptop and type in a few key words at a search engine such as Google or Bing. Then you start sifting through the results. An hour later, you're still in front of the screen, not much smarter about vacations in the south of France but still clicking and reading and clicking and reading. In fact, you may have completely forgotten about "vacations in France" and aimlessly wandered through countless other topics! If you're like millions of sentient adults with a laptop and wireless access, it's quite possible that this activity—mindless net-surfing—takes up more hours of your time than you realize or can afford to spare. But if you knew in advance that one hour later you would be evaluating your net-surfing according to how much short-term satisfaction and long-term benefit it provided you, I suspect it would either (a) make you think twice about going online in the first place, or (b) make you use your time online with more discipline and more focus on its short- and long-term benefits.

That's the power behind this exercise in self-directed follow-up. It not only tells us what's working after the fact, but it also makes us think about our actions *before the fact*.

I've recently adopted this method in regard to my own time surfing the Internet. Before I allow myself to get lost for an hour in a pointless cascade of links and screens, I now ask myself these two questions: "How much happiness am I going to get from the next hour? How much meaning will come from the next hour?" Sometimes I'll conclude that going online will deliver short-term satisfaction or long-term benefit—because I need the information and the search will be instructive. But many times I realize that I'll just be doing it as a low-strain alternative to getting back to more important activities. I'll be wasting my time. Whatever I conclude, the self-examination instructs my behavior: I either abandon the activity or find a way to extract more satisfaction and benefit from it.

It's such a simple strategy that it's tempting to discount its utility. But you'll be surprised at how effective it is in increasing the happiness and meaning in your life. Let me give you a couple of related examples:

I once had a CEO client who had a penchant for making sarcastic remarks to his employees. In his case, I abbreviated the two questions into a four-word test. Before he opened his mouth and said something that he would regret, I told him to ask himself, "Is it worth it?" He was skeptical at first. I explained that the question was like closing his office door when he didn't want to be interrupted. The door won't keep everybody out, but it makes people think twice before they knock. After twelve months of using this tactic, he made the startling admission that half the things he was going to say were "not worth saying." So he stopped saying them— and within a year he was perceived as a much more effective leader.

As I write this book, the global economy is highly uncertain. I always counsel my friends in major organizations, "This is not a great year to make 'ego points.'" One simple questioning activity that two of my friends swear has changed their lives—and led to major promotions—is to breathe before speaking and acting, then ask yourself, "Is what I am about to say or do in the best interest of myself and the people that I love?" If the answer is "no," think hard before saying or doing it!

This simple "two question" discipline can be applied to any activity. Imagine that you're about to attend a one-hour, mandatory meeting. Your initial mind-set is that the meeting will be a boring waste of time. But on this occasion, you flash forward an hour into the future and ask yourself two questions: *How much long-term benefit or meaning did I experience from this activity? How much short-term satisfaction or happiness did I experience in this activity?* Remember, it's your life. If the meeting makes you feel miserable and empty, it's *your* misery and emptiness. So try to make the best of the situation rather than defaulting to the role of victim. You have two options. Option A is to attend the meeting and be miserable (and probably assist other attendees in being miserable too). Option B is to make the meeting more meaningful and enjoyable. You might be able to do this by observing your colleagues more closely than ever, or by asking the attendees a question that you've been dying to ask, or by creatively generating an idea that becomes the inspiration for future progress. Your options are not as limited or limiting as you think. But you may never even consider these options without first posing the two questions.

All you're doing is changing how you approach any activity. You are changing your mindset. You're no longer defaulting to inertia—i.e., continuing to do what you've been doing. You're electing to be more mindful, more alert, and more awake. Remember this as you pursue the courses of action in this book. This is how we can overcome the pernicious effects of inertia, or mindless activity. This is how we can solve the Mojo Paradox. This is how we can regain control of our future and create positive change. This is how Mojo begins.

(Please go to MojoTheBook.com to download your "Mojo Meter." This fun, easy-to-use, and free application will enable you to monitor your experience of happiness and meaning as you journey through the day. By simply monitoring and reviewing your results—a process that will take only seconds of your time—you can begin to learn what matters and what doesn't really matter in your life.)

The Building Blocks of Mojo

CHAPTER 4

Identity: Who Do You Think You Are?

Before you can assess your Mojo—that positive spirit—toward what *you* are doing now—that starts from the inside—and radiates to the outside—you have to determine who "you" are. How do you define yourself?

Ask me this question concerning my profession—and my answer is simple and immediate: "I help successful people achieve positive, lasting change in behavior." That's a ten-word description of how I see myself as a professional that's so indelible it may as well be tattooed on my forehead.

I didn't always define myself this way.

When I was fourteen, I was "one of the boys" back in Kentucky. That's how I saw myself. A few years later, I was the first member of my family to graduate from college. By my late twenties, I had a Ph.D. in Organizational Behavior from UCLA under my belt and a teaching position at Loyola. I saw myself as a researcher and professor. It wasn't until my forties—more than half the average person's lifetime—that I could even approach a self-definition as pithy as "I help successful people achieve positive, lasting change in behavior."

Now, tell me: Who do *you* think *you* are?

Take your time. It's not a test with one correct answer. On the other hand, it's the kind of question that ends up stumping the vast majority of people.

Identity is a complicated subject, and we make it even more complicated when we're not sure where to look for the best answer. Many people hurtle back to their past—to signal events, memorable triumphs, painful disasters—in order to define themselves. Some rely on the testimony of others—a boss or teacher's good review—as a means of defining themselves.

Still others project themselves into the future, defining themselves as who they would like to be rather than who they actually are.

Let's take the complexity out of the question. Let's make it simple—so we can understand our identity and, in turn, do something about it.

At its core, our identity is determined by two dynamics complementing and competing with one another.

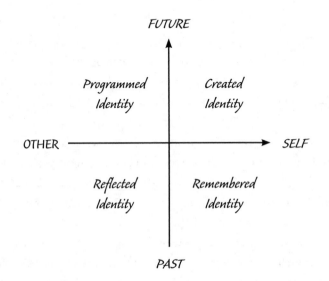

One vector represents the interplay between our *past* and our *future*. I spend a lot of my time admonishing clients to stop clinging to their past—and certainly to stop using the past as an excuse for current or future behavior—but there's no getting around the fact that much of our sense of self is determined by our past. How could it not be? Then again, if we want to make positive changes in our lives, we also need some sense of a future self—not the person we think we were but the person we want to become. This tug of war between our past and future selves, not surprisingly, can leave heads spinning as we veer between the comfort of our past self and the unknown promise of a future self.

The other vector tracks the tension between the image *others* have of us and our *self* image. It's the different weight we assign to what others say about us and what we tell ourselves.

Each of the four boxes created by this matrix represents one of four different sources of our identity. Each of these four sources of our identity combines to influence our Mojo.

1. Remembered Identity

In the lower-right-hand corner, where self and past collide, lies our *Remembered* Identity. How do you know who you are? Because you remember events in your life that helped form your sense of self. It's not so important whether these are glorious moments in your autobiography or events you'd rather erase; what's important is that you can't forget these touchstones. For better or worse, they've left an impact—and when you write a profile of yourself, these moments inevitably get reported.

The good news is that successful people, with robust senses of self-worth, tend to mine their past for the shiny diamonds, not the lumps of coal. They do this, in part, out of self-protection. After all, who in their right mind would gorge on painful or embarrassing episodes from his or her past, let alone allow these episodes to define his or her identity? The trouble is, the further you go back into your past, the greater the chances that your Remembered Identity doesn't match up with who you are today. The world is full of people who aced their teenage years, but is there a sadder commentary about an adult than "he peaked in high school"?

Likewise, the workplace is full of people who made mistakes in their past, but those errors do not necessarily pinpoint with any accuracy who they are now.

I remember asking one of my more self-effacing clients—a man with amazing achievements—to itemize his pluses and minuses as an executive.

"Well, I'm not very good at follow-up," he said.

"How do you know that?" I asked.

"My biggest screw-ups in business occurred when I didn't pay attention to my customers," he said. "I didn't check up on them as much as they'd like. I didn't return phone calls promptly. I didn't always do what I promised to do, at least not in the timely manner they expected. And sometimes I lost customers because of that."

I glanced down at the feedback I had gathered about the man from his direct reports and colleagues. He was a capable leader, with several thousand employees under his command. He had a few behavioral issues that needed to be dealt with, but "bad at follow-up" was not on the list.

"When was the last time a customer gave you negative feedback for poor follow-up?" I asked.

"It's been a while, at least ten years."

"Then why do you still insist you're bad at it?" I asked.

"I always remembered being bad at follow-up," he laughed.

That's where Remembered Identity can cheat us in establishing our Mojo. There's nothing wrong with harkening back to the past to sort out your strengths and weaknesses. But cling too tightly and you might be getting it all wrong, creating a dark blurry picture of someone who doesn't exist anymore.

2. Reflected Identity

In the lower-left-hand corner, where the past and other people's opinions meet, is *Reflected* Identity. Other people remember events in your past and they remind you of them, sometimes constantly. It's one thing for the executive above to admit to poor follow-up. But if his boss or wife or customers tell him the same thing, it reinforces the picture he already has of himself. You might know this as feedback. Feedback from others is how we shape our Reflected Identity.

As a professional who relies on feedback as a tool for helping people change for the better, I would never disparage its value. But I will mention that not all feedback is offered in good faith or in the most forgiving spirit.

It could be the spouse who keeps dredging up your one or two failures as a mate. It could be the colleague who never misses an opportunity to remind you of one of your workplace disasters. It could be the boss whose only impression of you is some less-than-brilliant statement you made in a meeting, which he repeats like a leitmotif whenever your name comes up. (I gave feedback to one manager who repeatedly derided one of his top lieutenant's work habits, all because the subordinate refused to schedule an early morning phone call with the boss over a holiday week-end. I regarded this as an admirable display of work-life balance, but the manager saw it as evidence of the man's 9-to-5 mentality and, therefore, a lack of commitment.) While some of our feedback may be quite fair, some of it may be part of the towel-snapping give-and-take of a lively corporate environment, where humor and piquant one-liners play key roles. But in an environment where we tend to become what other people say we are, the wrong kind of feedback can be self-limiting and pernicious.

People who keep reflecting your worst moments back to you—with the implication that these moments are the *real* you—are no different than the friend who sees that you're on a diet trying to lose weight and yet insists, "C'mon, you can loosen up for one day. Have a second helping of cake." They're trying to suck you back to a past self, someone you used to be, not who you are or want to become.

Yes, there's value in paying attention to your Reflected Identity—but healthy skepticism is called for here as well. At its worst, your Reflected Identity may be based on little more than hearsay and gossip. It may enhance your reputation or it may tarnish it. But either way, it's not necessarily a true reflection of who you are.

Even if your Reflected Identity is accurate, it doesn't have to be *predictive.* We can all change!

3. Programmed Identity

In the upper-left-hand corner is *Programmed* Identity, which is the result of other people sending messages about who you are or will become in the future. When I was growing up my mother imprinted me with two immutable notions—(1) I was smarter than all of the kids in the neighborhood and (2) I was a slob. The first notion, I now realize, was part of my mother's natural desire to have a successful son. The second was the distillate of my mother's own incredible need to be tidy and clean. After years of hearing this from my mother, I grew up with an outsized (and frankly delusional) faith in my own brainpower, and I was an incredible slob. My mother had programmed me to believe these attributes were integral components of what made me *me.* It wasn't until I started understanding the dynamics of identity that I began to realize: (1) I wasn't always that smart and (2) I didn't have to be a slob.

By the time I got to graduate school, I was shocked—shocked!—to learn that my professors and fellow students also had mothers, fathers, and other important people telling them how smart they were, and, to my dismay, they seemed to be smarter than me. I had to rethink my mother's programming. I also, if only to improve my odds on getting a date, worked on not being such a slob.

Even in its most extreme forms, there can be a lot that is positive about Programmed Identity. For example, the Marine Corps excels at forging new identities for its recruits—and it does so in the relatively short span of eight weeks at boot camp. That's where new recruits are literally drilled into thinking of themselves not only as soldiers but as members of a unit—so that they have their comrades' backs at all times and perform fearlessly under the stress of combat. It's the reason Marines get "Semper Fi" tattoos and regard being a Marine as part of their identity for life. It's the reason that wounded soldiers who've been sent stateside for medical attention want to get back to their unit as soon as they're healed; they want to be a part of something bigger than themselves. That's how they've been trained. The Corps is at the core of their identity.

Your Programmed Identity has many sources. It can be influenced by the profession you enter, or the culture you grew up in, or the company you work for, or the entire industry you work in, or the people you select as your trusted friends. Each of these can shape your opinion of yourself, some more vividly than you may realize.

Not long ago I met up with an old friend from graduate school whom I hadn't seen for years. I remembered him as a quiet, earnest academic type who liked nothing more than dreaming up clever social experiments and writing research papers about them. Then he decided he needed more money than a life in academe would provide, so he became a trader on Wall Street. I caught up with him a few years into his new career, and the change in his personality was impossible to ignore. He was very aggressive and clearly cared a lot about making money.

"You've come a long way since the psych lab," I said, trying to make a joke about the "new" person sitting in front of me.

"It's the culture," he said. "Everyone in my company is there for only one reason: to make money. I was told that in order to succeed in this environment, I would need to become like everyone else. I guess that I have."

In other words, he didn't disagree that he was a changed man, or that this change was not all positive. He simply gave himself a free pass by defining his new personality by his industry "programming."

And therein lies the flaw in our eager acceptance of our Programmed Identity. It can become a convenient scapegoat for our behavioral mistakes.

I was once hired to work with a Greek-American executive whose scores on showing respect for colleagues and subordinates were abysmal. As I reviewed his coworkers' feedback with him, his first comment was, "I don't know if you've ever worked with men from Greece before—"

I cut him off and said, "I've worked with a lot of men from Greece, and most of them were not perceived as mean or disrespectful. Don't blame your problems on Socrates!" In effect, he was blaming his supposed cultural heritage—his alleged programming—for his acting like a jerk.

Through the years I've become a connoisseur of people using their "programming" as an excuse. I've heard overbearing people who always need to get their own way blame the parents who spoiled them and gave them everything they wanted (Blame My Parental programming). I've heard overweight people blame their inability to shed pounds on their genetic makeup (Blame My Genetic programming). I've heard bigots blame their intolerance on the hateful small-minded town where they were raised (Blame My Neighbors' programming). I've heard aggressive don't-get-in-my-way salespeople blame their boorish behavior on their company's ruthless Darwinian culture (Blame My Company's programming).

At some point, usually when we've suffered an unambiguous Nojo moment for the second or third time (e.g., getting fired or passed over for a promotion again) it finally dawns on us that maybe we can't lay all our problems on our programming. That's when we stop turning to the past and to others for our sense of self and look to our . . .

4. Created Identity

In the upper-right-hand corner of our matrix, where *self* and *future* meet, is your *Created* Identity. Our Created Identity is the identity that we decide to create for ourselves. It is the part of our identity that is not controlled by our past or by other people. The most truly successful people that I have met have created identities to become the human beings that *they* chose to be—without being slaves to the past or to other people. This concept is the beating heart of Mojo.

In my job as an executive coach, I help my successful clients achieve positive, lasting change in *behavior*. As I have grown older, I now realize that I often should be helping them change their *identity*—the way they define themselves. If we change our behavior, but don't change our identity, we may feel "phony" or "unreal," no matter how much we achieve. If we change our behavior *and* change the way we define ourselves, we can be both *different* and *authentic* at the same time.

I am not naïve. I don't believe that we can become *anything* that we want just because we choose to do it. I am never going to be a professional basketball player. No matter how many positive thoughts I may have, LeBron James and Kobe Bryant have little to fear. We all have real physical, environmental, or mental limitations that we may never be able to overcome. My extensive research has indicated that we will all get old and die. We cannot wish physical reality away with "positive thinking."

On the other hand, I am amazed at what we *can* change if we do not artificially limit ourselves. In my own work, I have seen leaders make massive positive changes, both in the way that they treat others and the way that they see themselves. Everything that follows in this book is based upon these experiences and my belief that most of us can change both our behaviors and our identities.

Our Created Identity allows us to become a different person. We can change to fit changing times. We can change to achieve higher goals.

I had a wonderful experience in meeting a person who has radically changed his identity over the years when, at dinner one night, I happened to be seated next to Bono, the lead singer of the Irish mega-band U2.

I didn't know much about Bono at the time. As an "older guy," I was a little embarrassed by the fact that I knew his name but was not familiar with any of his records (since they had been made after 1975). Someone told me that he was one of the top rock stars in the world. It was interesting to me that a star of this magnitude was asked to speak—not about music—but about his ideas for making our world a better place.

Fortunately for me, he didn't ask me about any of his records. We just talked about life. In a way, it shouldn't have been surprising to me that

Bono thought about his identity. Successful musicians, who can continue to fill arenas for three decades, finding new audiences while keeping old fans, are masters at creating and managing their identities. I guess if someone is plastering your image on posters, CDs, and T-shirts, you have to control your identity—or someone else will.

I learned a lot from Bono's personal story. He is a wonderful example of a person who has been able to change his identity and—at the same time—remain true to himself.

In his early years, Bono's identity was "regular guy," just a bloke from Dublin who liked hanging around with his mates. From our conversation, it didn't sound as if he had fully shed the "regular guy" identity—or wanted to. He apologized to me for using multiple variations on the "F-word." (I assured him that his language did not trouble me. As a teenager back in Kentucky, I thought the "F-word" was the adjective that preceded most nouns.) For all of his fame and money, Bono still impressed me as a regular guy. He did not act pretentious. He was not overly sold on how wonderful he was. He was courteous enough to be concerned about possibly offending some white-haired, nearly bald guy that he had never met.

After defining himself as a "regular guy," Bono became a "rock and roll fan." Like many kids his age, he fell in love with music. He was animated in his discussion of the musicians who had influenced his life—and how much he enjoyed listening to them as a youth. He talked about how he still loved listening to new groups.

Bono's next identity was "musician." He described how he had made a commitment to his craft and how lucky he was to find something he loved to do. He talked about the innocent joy of forming a band with friends when no status or money was involved. It was clear from his description that he not only loved being a musician then—he still loved it. He doesn't make music just to make money—he makes music just to make music!

At this point, Bono was describing the familiar trajectory of every young boy who dreams of being a star. What happened next was a long shot. He went from being a "musician" to being a "rock star." He clearly liked being a rock star. He enjoyed the life, the fans, and the access to influential people. He referred to himself as a "rock star" when we talked. I realized that he was using the phrase with a very useful detachment, as if it was the only way to accurately describe the one-in-a-zillion situation he found himself in. Beyond the view of an adoring public, he was still a regular guy, with a wife and four kids at home. But when he was in public, his identity was clearly labeled "rock star"—and, without being arrogant, he was smart enough to recognize that this is an important part of his identity.

As much as he remained a sum of all his other identities—regular guy, rock 'n' roll fan, musician, rock star—it was evident that Bono was forging a new identity as a humanitarian, and that he was as professional and serious about this new identity as anything else in his life—maybe even more!

He recounted with deep feeling his experience of visiting Africa during the great famine of the 1980s. He talked about his lobbying of political leaders to reduce African debt. He talked about his desire to alleviate human suffering. There was no doubt that a big chunk of his remaining years would be devoted to doing whatever he could to make our world a better place.

As it turns out, my friend Richard Schubert was CEO of the American Red Cross during the great African famine of the 1980s. Richard gave me the opportunity to go on a volunteer mission to Africa at the same time Bono was there. This was—and still is—the most unforgettable trip of my life. In my nine days there I saw many people starving to death. I saw the hard work that was being done by wonderful humanitarians to save as many people as they could.

Tears came to my eyes as Bono described his experience during the African famine—and I remembered my experience.

Although I didn't own any of his records, it turns out we did have something in common.

In his after-dinner speech, Bono did not take cheap shots at politicians, governments, or anyone else—even when several politically charged questions from the audience made the opportunity very tempting. He was clearly there to raise money, not to appease one side's political views over another. His desire to help others far exceeded his need to be smart or fashionable. He is a man with a mission. He isn't pretending to be a humanitarian. He is a humanitarian, and he is incredibly disciplined about how he presents this newfound identity to the world. His mission was clearly more important than his ego.

After that dinner, I couldn't help thinking how extraordinary Bono's analysis of his identity was.

At first blush, it may not appear to be much of an achievement. After all, Bono is rich; he can afford to take a sabbatical from rock 'n' roll and pursue his humanitarian interests. Bono is also a celebrity, which provides him with a loud megaphone to voice his opinions. He's also a successful creative artist, which automatically provides him with a large receptive audience for what comes out of that megaphone.

But on closer inspection, at least in terms of creating a new identity, Bono's celebrity is a double-edged sword. A lot of people are very hostile to the idea of celebrated people moving from their primary sphere of influence (e.g., movies, music, or sports) to an unrelated, more "serious" realm of public discourse. Think of all those stars—Angelina Jolie (on the left) or the late Charlton Heston (on the right)—who are mocked as much as they are admired for voicing a political opinion or trying to help people. Stick to your day job, they're told, as fans and media question their motives and commitment. Bono also faced the additional hurdle of being part of a large thriving enterprise, namely U2. What if his three lifelong band mates resented his utopian dreams or thought his mission threatened the band? These are not questions to be treated lightly. Bono not only had to create an identity for himself, he had to earn support from his fellow band members.

In that context, Bono's self-transformation is actually amazing. He did not let his definition of who he was—attractive as the identity of "rock star" may be—limit his potential for what else he could become. Frankly, I'd argue that creating a new identity is more difficult for Bono *because* of his celebrity than it is for average civilians like you and me. We don't have as much to lose, or as firmly established an image to shed. And we don't have hundreds of thousands of fans questioning our right to do so.

More than anything, Bono's example is inspiring. Many of us make the mistake of treating our identity as a fixed, immutable object. We believe it cannot be altered, at least not significantly. As a result, we never try to create a new identity. One of the greatest obstacles to changing our Mojo is here—in the paralysis we create with self-limiting definitions of who we are.

All of us do this in some way. The client who hangs on to the self-image that he's bad at follow-up, long after it's true or meaningful, is literally living with a false identity. So is the boor who thinks his cultural heritage excuses his rough manner, although he's only fooling himself with this fake ID. But the real damage is how these limiting IDs prevent us from changing—and becoming someone better than we used to be.

When we define ourselves by saying we are deficient at some activity, we tend to create the reality that proves our definition. I once heard a client claim that he made a bad first impression. As someone who was favorably impressed by his manner the *first* time I met him, I asked, "What do you do the *second time* that reverses the bad first impression?" The conversation that followed was surreal.

"I'm much looser with people the second time," he said.

"Why?" I asked.

"I know them a little better, so I talk more freely, I joke around. I'm confident that I can charm them."

"Why can't you do that the first time?" I asked.

"I'm shy. Being outgoing with strangers just wouldn't be me."

"And yet, that is who you are the second time," I said. "Don't you find that odd?"

"I've always been like that," he said, as if that ended the matter, as if he was beyond forming a new version of himself with strangers.

This client was indulging in the most transparent form of self-limiting behavior, relying on crude circular logic to prove his point. He literally stopped trying to win people over on first meeting because he defined himself as being bad at first impressions. It boggled my mind. But many of us are no different. When we tell ourselves that we can't sell, or are awful at speaking in public, or don't listen well, we usually find a way to fulfill our prophecy. We literally groom ourselves to fail.

In summary, how do we know who we are? Our identities are *remembered, reflected, programmed,* and *created.* My suggestion to you is simple. First, review the various components of your current identity. Where did they originate? Then, review the matrix in the context of how you see yourself today—and who you would like to become in the future. If your present identity is fine with you, just work on becoming an even better version of who you are. If you want to make a change in your identity, be open to the fact that you may be able to change more than you originally believed that you could. Assuming that you do not have "incurable" or "unchangeable" limitations, you, like Bono, can create a new identity for your future, without sacrificing your past.

Your Mojo is that positive spirit toward what *you* are doing now that starts from the inside and radiates to the outside. To understand how you are relating to any activity, you need to understand your identity—who *you* are. To change your Mojo, you may need to either create a new identity for yourself or rediscover an identity that you have lost.

CHAPTER 5

Achievement: What Have You Done Lately?

Our achievements are the second component in creating our Mojo.

We tend to gauge our achievements by using two differing criteria. On the one hand, there are the accomplishments that make others aware of our ability and result in their recognizing us. This is what most people think about when they discuss achievement. On the other hand, there are the accomplishments that only we are aware of, related to our own abilities, that make us feel good about ourselves. Both are legitimate in their own way.

As we discussed earlier, our *Professional Mojo* is what we bring to the job. If we have the motivation, ability (or skill), understanding (or knowledge), confidence, and authenticity needed to excel, we will be "winners" in terms of achieving goals.

Our *Personal Mojo* is what the job brings to us. If we find happiness, meaning, reward, learning, and gratitude in what we are doing—we will define ourselves as "winners."

Both *Professional* and *Personal Mojo* are connected to achievement— just two different types of achievement.

In the "best of all worlds," the two types of achievement could be the same—what we do that impresses others makes us feel great about ourselves. But it doesn't always work out that way. Sometimes we perform magnificently at work, to great acclaim, but it doesn't elevate how we feel about ourselves. Sometimes we do something wonderful for the world and no one else is impressed.

It's easy to cite examples of achievements that make others aware of our ability. It happens every time we do something that's measured or rated by someone else. The most extreme example is the work of professional athletes. If you're a baseball player, your career is bulging with metrics that indicate how you're doing, from your batting average to your fielding percentage to your performance with runners in scoring position and so on ad infinitum. If it happens anywhere near the ballpark, baseball's obsessive statisticians have found a way to measure it.

CEOs are almost in the same league as athletes. From their companies' recent gain or loss in stock price, to earnings per share, to return on investment, to market share, to EBIDTA—everything they do gets the scoreboard treatment, flashing the news of their performance to everyone.

Investment bankers, stock and bond traders, and other financial engineers are just a notch below athletes and CEOs in the assessment of their achievements. They measure their ability by how much money they're making for their clients and themselves. The more they make, the better.

The metrics to determine "What have you done lately?" are all around us. People selling cars answer the question based on how many cars they've sold in the recent quarter (and chances are there's a scoreboard in the manager's office that shows just how well those salespeople are performing vis-à-vis their peers at the dealership). A magazine salesperson can flip through a recent issue and literally count the ads he or she has sold that month. A real estate broker can look at a map and see how many homes he or she has closed on—and how many remain unsold. An insurance claims adjuster can add up how many claims he or she has settled in the past month. In one way or another, there's always a metric hovering over what we do, whether it's a retail manager scanning the racks and shelves for what's selling, or it's the Detroit assembly-line worker who knows a steering mechanism must be installed on a truck every ninety-five seconds.

But what if someone else's yardstick isn't how *you* measure what you've done lately? What if making others aware of your ability isn't your driving force?

That's when the second criterion kicks in: You value your achievements based on how good you feel about yourself and what you're doing.

Humanitarians are the most extreme example of this. If they're fighting hunger or disease in Africa, they're not doing it to impress others with their "humanitarian skill set." They're not doing it to land a better job after their detour in Africa. Frankly, few people are paying attention to what they're doing. Doing humanitarian work is what they do, with or without anyone else watching, because it helps others and, in turn, makes them feel good about the life they've chosen.

Teachers, police officers, firefighters, and social workers are not much different. They don't go into these jobs for the money. For the most part, they don't do it for the glory and applause. Yes, there's careerism—a competitive urge to impress others in order to climb up the ladder—in these jobs, but it's not the dominant force. In many cases, their self-assessment of how well they do the job is more meaningful to these people than what their superiors think. They do these jobs to serve others in their community. That invests the job with purpose and meaning. That's why they feel good about it.

Musicians, writers, and artists fit the mold too. The odds of "making it" (whatever that means) in any of these pursuits are so long—a million to one—that it's amazing anyone sticks with them. Actors may be the most egregious cohort of people who do what they do because it makes them feel good about themselves. Yes, actors love the spotlight and get onstage because they want to impress others with their ability. But if you've ever met an actor, professional or amateur, you know that validation in the form of praise or a standing ovation is not their primary motivating force. After all, even when the critics blast them for their performance and audiences yawn (the purest illustration of failing to impress others with your ability), actors continue to pursue their craft—because they feel good doing it. To them acting is its own reward.

I'm not judging any of these people. The hedge fund manager who answers "What have you done lately?" by privately calculating his net worth or by citing that his fund is up 12 percent above alpha for the year is no less authentic than the relief worker who answers the same question by telling herself, "I save lives." For some people, meaning and happiness revolve around financial security. Other people find meaning in helping others. If people pursue either of these goals with clarity of purpose—in other words, they know exactly what they're doing and they're not pretending otherwise—they will have all the Mojo they need.

The Disconnect Between
Their Definition of Achievement and
Our Definition of Achievement

A Mojo crisis can sometimes arise when there is a disconnect between the two criteria we use to measure our achievement—when what others feel about our accomplishments is not in sync with what we feel about them ourselves.

I see this all the time in my work. Consider Richard, a corporate communications executive. On the surface, Richard has an interesting and challenging job. He manages delicate investor relations. He appears on radio and television to spin his company's message. He gets to parry with all those pesky journalists who write about his company and his CEO. The job is rich and varied, calling for creativity and adaptability—and there's sometimes even a hint of glamour. At any rate, it's never dull. Plus, he's very good at what he does, so good that his CEO regards him as "indispensable" and pays him accordingly. In other words, if Richard defined achievement by how well he impressed people with his abundant skills, he would think of himself as a raging success.

But Richard doesn't consider himself a real achiever. Yes, he has the trappings of success: the corporate power and prestige and all the accoutrements that a big paycheck can provide. The only problem is he has always considered corporate communications a fallback career. In his mind, he's a creative wordsmith. He wrote plays and short stories in college. And now, more than twenty years into his career, he regards much of what he does, especially the press releases and speechwriting, as a form of intellectual slumming. What he really wants to be is a full-time writer. He wants to shuck the job and stay home writing novels.

"So quit," I told him. "Go home and write your novels."

I was hoping he would, but I knew he wouldn't. If Richard truly had the courage to act on the fact that writing fiction was his calling, he would have done it long ago. His day job wasn't stopping him. In fact, it could be argued that his lucrative day job afforded him the luxury of following his muse. It paid the bills, put a roof over his family's head, and gave him the satisfaction of being a good provider. With all that real and psychic sustenance from his corporate job, what was stopping him from spending his evenings or weekends writing his novel? What was preventing him from getting up early each morning and spending an hour or two of quiet time on his writing?

I don't know the answer to that one (although I would guess that a lack of discipline plays a big part). What I do know is that Richard was seriously Mojo-challenged. He didn't feel a positive spirit toward what he was doing, and yet his job required him to register a positive attitude among his bosses and peers. All of which made him feel like a phony. And he knew it, which in turn made him even more miserable.

Richard experienced a classic Mojo dilemma—the mismatch between what he was giving to his job and what his job was giving to him—the disconnect between how the world defined "achievement" for him and how he defined "achievement" for himself.

Those opposing notions created a hope that Richard clung to like a life preserver: that he would eventually have a professional life devoted exclusively to writing fiction and that this "new life" would finally bring him meaning and happiness.

Of course, Richard will never know if that belief is true unless he takes a chance and does something about it. Until then, it's just a dream. And Richard will remain in a state of limbo, denying that it's just a dream, and pretending that it's a real option. It's a core belief through which he interprets everything that happens to him.

Unfortunately, Richard is hardly an unusual case study. Every day I encounter people who feel trapped. They are high achievers as defined by the world, but not by themselves. Their very "achievement" leads to recognition that is almost impossible to abandon.

On the other hand, Richard's opposite, Mary, has a mirror image Mojo dilemma.

Mary went into social work to make a positive difference. She knew that she would never make the same kind of money as her friends and, when she first entered the field, it didn't bother her. As the years wore on, however, she started to become bitter. She believed that she was indeed helping others and making a positive difference. What "frosted" her was illustrated by her interactions at her high school reunion. She was incredibly annoyed that many of her classmates were living in bigger homes and wearing nicer clothes that she was. What made it even worse was that she considered most of these people to be "down the food chain" from her in intelligence and work ethic. There they were, with less brain power and making no real contribution to the world, yet looking down on her, as if she were inferior to them!

As Mary grew older, she was succeeding in making herself more and more miserable.

Mary and Richard illustrate two sides of the same coin. Richard's Mojo is challenged because the world sees him as a high achiever and recognizes him for it. He is trapped because he discounts his own achievement—and does not believe that what he is doing is meaningful. Mary's Mojo is challenged because the world sees her as a low achiever and does not give her the recognition she thinks she deserves. She is trapped because she cannot discount the world's opinion in spite of the fact that she believes what she is doing is truly meaningful.

Think of your own definition of "achievement." What matters to you? What matters to the world? Be honest with yourself. Look in the mirror. Make peace with your true motivations. Try not to go through life deluding yourself by pretending that when the world cares, you do—or pretending that when the world does not care, you do not care.

Are We Kidding Ourselves?

Are we kidding ourselves? I face this every day when I pose "What have you done lately?" to people I meet. If we are not careful, our answers can be a virtual catalog of delusional thinking.

One of the biggest mistakes high achievers make is in overestimating our contribution to a success, thus crediting ourselves with an achievement that does not rightly belong to us. When was the last time you heard a colleague recount a triumph that you recall as a team effort but, having gone through the rinse cycle of your colleague's ego, has ended up sounding like a one-man show?

On too many occasions, when we're not erasing our coworkers from the picture, we can find other ways to exaggerate the magnitude of our own achievements. We may think that our accomplishment has the impact of a nuclear bomb resonating throughout the company, when in fact it's more like a popgun barely making a sound. How often have you heard a colleague regale you with a blow-by-blow account of a sale, or a meeting with a client, while you politely listen, and think, *So what?*

People also go too far back in time, digging up an achievement that happened so long ago that it's no longer relevant and may even qualify as ancient history. It makes them sound as if they're clinging to their past or, worse, haven't done anything significant in a long, long time.

The opposite is also true. A lot of us tend to cite our most recent achievement, as if an event has more weight or significance because it is freshest in our minds. Psychologists call this "recency bias." It's why a gambler doubles his bet at a blackjack table after he's won a few hands; he overweights his feeling of good luck, even though his odds of winning haven't changed. It's why investors plunge into a stock or mutual fund based on the most recent quarterly performance, even though a more reliable time frame would be five- or ten-year performance. It's why so many Americans feared another attack immediately after 9/11, but the farther removed we are from the events of 2001, the less we fear a reprise of what happened. It's tempting, almost irresistible, to gravitate to the nearest example at hand to calculate our achievements, but it may not be the most meaningful representation of our abilities.

Remember this as you establish what you have done lately. Apply a stress test to each achievement by asking yourself:

- Is this what happened or am I filtering it through some inflexible personal preconception or belief?

- Am I exaggerating my role in the achievement?

- Am I discounting other people's contribution?

- Am I going too far back in time, so the achievement is no longer credible, it's just old?

- Am I attaching too much weight to a recent event simply because I remember it more vividly than an older event?

Chip away at the false assumptions that distort your achievements and you'll get a much clearer picture of what you've done lately. Without it, you'll never be able to envision everything else you can do.

By increasing our understanding of achievement—what it means to us and what it means to the world—we can increase our Mojo. We can look at ourselves more objectively. We can determine what really matters in our lives. We can strive for achievement that really matters to us—and let go of achievement that does not create happiness and meaning in our lives. If we want to increase our Mojo, we can either change the degree of our achievement—how well we are doing—or change the definition of our achievement—what we are trying to do well.

CHAPTER 6

Reputation: Who Do People Think You Are?

Reputation is the third element in establishing your Mojo. It's where you add up who you are (identity) and what you've done (achievement) and toss the combined sum out into the world to see how people respond. Your reputation is people's recognition—or rejection—of your identity and achievement. Sometimes you'll agree with the world's opinion. Sometimes you won't. But many times you may not even be aware of it. You cannot create your reputation by yourself (the rest of the world, by definition, always has something to say about it). But you can influence it—and in this chapter we'll discuss how you can do that and how it affects your Mojo.

We often want to believe that we have "character" that is different than reputation. We define our character as "who we really are" and our reputation as "who other people think we really are." In situations where their assessment is different than our own, we generally define the assessment of others as "wrong." It takes courage to realize that, in some cases, other people's view of us may be just as accurate—or even more so—than our view of ourselves.

We often do not know what our reputation is. We're fairly clear-eyed about what we think of other people. But when it comes to what they think of us, we can live in the dark. We may have no clue about what other people are saying about us behind our back, and therefore no opportunity to correct falsehoods (if they are inaccurate) or mend our ways (if they are correct). This is one reason, in my experience, that reputation is such a neglected component in our Mojo makeup: We don't have enough information to do much about it. So we ignore it.

I know this is true from my one-on-one coaching work with executives who want to change their behavior. The first thing I do is conduct a

360-degree feedback assessment of the executive's behavior on the job (in some cases, this is the first time the executive has ever been "reviewed" by people below rather than above him or her). I interview fifteen to twenty colleagues and direct reports. I tally up the comments and report what I've found. In a few cases, much of what I uncover is breaking news to the executive. He or she will express complete surprise and then utter some variation on "Really, people think I'm _____ (fill in the blank)?"

These are smart, successful, motivated individuals. They've reached their incredible position in life by being attuned to what other people think of them—and thoughtfully adjusting their behavior accordingly. And yet my "polling" results on their reputation are often an eye-opener for them. If these hyper-successful professionals are sometimes in the dark about their reputation, it's not surprising that the rest of us can be clueless.

Quick question: Amid all your list-making and organizing and planning your next moves, when was the last time you sat down and thought about your reputation?

The likely truth is that unless you're a celebrity, politician, or other kind of public figure—people whose reputations are constantly being assessed, elevated, and diminished in the media—you've never codified your reputation at work. Never written down what you thought it might be, or what you want it to be. Never asked your colleagues for feedback about it. Never even thought about what you must do to establish it. At best, you may harbor a vague notion that you have a reputation for "being a nice person," or "being good at my job," or "being willing to help out." But that's about it. You've never dug deeper into the specific personality traits, skills, behaviors, and accomplishments that help form a reputation.

Would You Rather Be "Smart" or "Effective"?

It's taken me a while to figure out why so many of us neglect our reputation. It's not that we don't care. We care a lot. It's that we confuse our need to *consider ourselves to be smart* with our need to *be considered effective by the world*. The two are not the same thing, and one often overwhelms the other.

One of the most pernicious impulses among successful people is our overwhelming need to prove how smart we are. It's drilled into us from our earliest school days, when we're graded and ranked and bell-curved in a winnowing process that separates the average from the smart from the super-smart. It continues through high school and college and graduate school, where it's even more deeply ingrained because we think the competition to be smart suddenly has lifelong consequences. And we continue this competition into the workplace, although our "report cards" now come in the form of promotions, paychecks, and praise rather than test-score percentiles. We want our bosses and colleagues to admire our brainpower.

I say it's pernicious because the need to be the "smartest person in the room" often leads to some incredibly stupid behavior. It leads to dumb arguments, in which we fight to prove that we're right and someone else is wrong. It's the reason we feel the need to tell someone who shares valuable information with us that we "already knew that"—though it devalues them. It's the reason we will fight to the death to defend an opinion or decision that has worn out its welcome. It's the reason bosses can't resist improving a subordinate's idea by saying, "That's great but it would be even better if you . . ." Frankly, it's one of the reasons so many of us are such poor listeners. We're so invested in presenting ourselves as smart that we believe we don't need to hear everything that people tell us; we're smart enough to tune out people and still succeed.

Not everyone behaves like this. There are people who are willing to sacrifice the fleeting buzz of needing to be smart for the more valuable feeling of being effective—of delivering on time, of bringing out the best in others, of finding the simplest route to a solution.

To find out which side you fall on—smart or effective—consider this hypothetical, which I call the Brain Pill Question:*

You are offered a Brain Pill. If you swallow this pill, you will become 10 percent more intelligent than you currently are; you will be more adept at reading comprehension, logic, and critical thinking. However, to all other people you know (and to all future

* I owe this puzzler to the writer Chuck Klosterman, who posed it for different purposes in his journalism collection *IV* (Scribner, 2007).

people you meet), you will seem 20 percent less intelligent. In other words, you will immediately become smarter, but the rest of the world will perceive you as dumber (and there is no way you can ever alter the universality of that perception). Do you take this pill?

Your answer says a lot about how you value your reputation. A lot of people would take the pill, happy to have the added brainpower—and to hell with the world's diminished opinion.

Personally, I wouldn't take the pill. It's not that I'm smug and self-satisfied with my brainpower as is. It's that I don't feel that the incremental gain of 10 percent in smarts is worth the 20 percent reduction in how my intelligence is perceived by the world. All I've done is create a 30 percent gap between how smart I think I am and what everyone else thinks. That's a big gap, providing a major blow to my reputation and an unwelcome load of professional frustration. After all, what's more frustrating than believing you're smart, yet being powerless to impact a world that believes you are not?

Let's take the Brain Pill Question out of the realm of the hypothetical. Let's say you're a design engineer, developing a product for your company. Engineers constantly face the choice of doing something brilliant or doing something practical. In this case, you can propose either an elegant solution that will be rejected by the company (because of costs or production difficulties or whatever) or a solution that is 20 percent worse but will be accepted. Which would you prefer? Do you want to be known as someone who builds elegant objects that never get made or as someone who provides practical solutions that always "ship out the door"? There's no correct answer here. Some people won't compromise their talent or principles to be more effective; some people will.

What I'd like to suggest here is that we shouldn't think of these decisions in terms of compromise. That suggests an inauthentic choice, something that's not true to our beliefs and goals. Instead, I'd like to posit that these choices are easier to understand and make *if* we have a clearer idea of the reputation we're trying to build for ourselves.

Personally, I'm in a position in my career where I can do a lot to shape my reputation. I write books, articles, and blogs (for *Harvard*

Business, BusinessWeek, and *The Huffington Post*) and give speeches and interviews, all of which allow me to deliver a thoughtful message about the reputation I want for myself. I'm also clear about what I want my reputation to be. I want people to think of me as someone who's extremely effective in helping successful leaders achieve positive, lasting change in behavior. I don't want to be just *good* in my field. I want a reputation as one of the *best.* Nothing wrong with that. It's no different than an athlete training for an Olympic gold medal. It's ambitious, but not unrealistic. Of course, I can't claim that reputation for myself in what I say (that would be meaningless, since anyone can score high on a self-assessment). I can suggest it as my goal (as I'm doing in this paragraph), but "at the end of the day" I have to earn it through the results I deliver. To be considered one of the best, I don't have a high margin for error.

Partly because of my reputational goal, many decisions in my career boil down to: Will it make me look smarter or make me become more effective? I always vote for *effective.* I'm not looking to be known as the smartest person with the most sophisticated theory about helping people change. I want to be known as the guy who is actually very effective at helping people change.

For example, many years ago, I was asked to work one-on-one with a senior executive at one of the largest and most admired companies in the world. I had worked at fairly big companies before, but this was far and away the biggest, most prestigious assignment of my life. The people I'd be working with would position me on a whole new level. The fact that this benchmark company called me instead of another executive coach was not only flattering but proof that I was nearing my target reputation. The executive in question was a smart, motivated, high-performing, deliver-the-numbers, arrogant know-it-all who got near the top of the corporate pyramid despite some pretty serious interpersonal flaws. He also was in charge of the company's most profitable division, which should have made him a corporate MVP and first in line to succeed the CEO. My job was to see if I could smooth out some of his rough behavioral edges, which in turn might provide him with a smoother glide in the CEO succession derby.

I conducted my usual 360-degree feedback interviews with the executive's colleagues. Then I discussed the results with him, at which point I was met with a brusque brush-off, suggesting that no matter what I said, this man would never accept that he needed to change. He just didn't care.

That's when I had a choice to make. Do I accept the assignment or walk away? A part of me—the part that wanted the top people at the company to think I was smart enough to run with their crowd—was tempted to take it on. Success would be a long shot. But hey, I told myself, no risk, no reward.

Another part of me—the part that kept its eye on my reputational objectives—knew I would be jumping into an empty grave if I worked with this impossible executive. If I couldn't actually help him change I would fail the assignment, which in turn would brand me as ineffective and might harm my reputation. I realized that this client did not really want to change—and that there was nothing that I was going to do about it.

In the end, I walked away, but not before telling the CEO my reasons. I don't think my reputation was harmed by any of this. And the irony wasn't lost on me: On its surface, walking away might have been an admission that I wasn't up to the task, but in fact in terms of advancing my career and maintaining my Mojo, it was the smartest thing I could do. (As it turned out, this executive was later dismissed by the company—and I was thanked by the CEO for having the courage to walk away from a potentially lucrative coaching assignment.)

Smart or effective? When you have to choose and your reputation is on the line, opting for the latter may actually cement the former.

Remember this smart/effective distinction the next time you face a career decision. Many of us, as I mentioned, are clueless about our reputations, so it makes sense that even fewer of us think about the long-term reputational impact when we make a decision. We're thinking short-term needs instead: Does my choice "take it to the next step," or make me look proactive, or get my boss off my back, or bring in some quick cash, or make me look like I'm outrunning my peers? These are all variations on the same question: "Am I smart enough?" It's not the same question as "Does this choice add or detract from my long-term reputation?" That's a different criterion altogether. From my experience, choosing to be effective rather than smart ultimately pays off in our reputation, our achievement, *and* our Mojo.

Why We May Be Clueless
About Our Reputations

The connection between your reputation and Mojo should be self-evident. After all, what people think of you affects how you feel about yourself. If people shower you with their good opinion—and you're aware of it—it can't help but lift your spirit. And you'll radiate that positive spirit back to them, all of which is the essence of Mojo.

This tranparency may not be the same when people have a bad opinion of us. A negative opinion is usually left unexpressed rather than shared (under the polite theory that "If you can't say something nice, say nothing at all"). So we're often not aware what people *really* think of us— and therefore unaware of the many ways that our reputation is being formed through misinformation or misinterpretation.

For one thing, in forming an opinion of you, people usually bring their own agenda to any interpretation of your actions. If you do something that affects them in a negative way, however proper, well intentioned, or for the greater good it may actually be, that negative impact will color their opinion of your action. Have you ever tried to help someone, only to have your efforts end up being resented or misinterpreted by the person you were trying to help? For example, you invite a colleague to join your group on a project, thinking he or she would like to be included in an opportunity to work on something different, whereas the object of your kind attention thinks you're piling on the work or scheming to get him or her to do your job. What you intended as genuine helpfulness comes off as meddling to someone else. We cannot predict with perfect certainty how people will respond to us or what we do. If we could, we'd never have to employ the apologetic phrase "I was only trying to help."

Our actions are also distorted by people's acceptance of the "conventional wisdom" about us—through what they've heard or casually observed firsthand. It is the filter through which they interpret our actions. This isn't necessarily bad, and can work to our advantage. If you're in any public forum where you are perceived as the most authoritative voice on a particular subject, you will be accorded a greater level of deference by others in the room, no matter how inane or misguided your comments—at least initially. Continue the trend by stringing together several silly comments in a row and even the least knowledgeable person in the room will begin to question your perceived "authority."

The flip side is also true. If people have heard bad things about you, they'll be looking for signs of bad behavior. Even when you fail to sink to their very low expectations, they may put a negative spin on behavior that they would otherwise excuse in someone with a more positive reputation. If people have heard that you are a "difficult person," that's the prism through which they'll interpret your actions. You may be in a meeting thinking you're engaging in a healthy—and much needed—debate about a decision, while all the others at the meeting, already predisposed to seeing you as "difficult," are indulgently nodding their heads and thinking, *What a jerk*.

These nuances of interpersonal dynamics—mostly other people's preconceptions—help mold our reputation. Taken in small doses, their impact is limited. But if we allow them to accumulate unchecked over time—through our ignorance or neglect—they inevitably become a "reality" we have to deal with.

That's when we must confront the million-dollar question: Can you form or change your reputation?

The short answer is yes. But it's not easy and it takes time.

The first thing to know is that your reputation is rarely if ever formed by a one-time catastrophic event—people can be extremely forgiving. Screw up once in a major way and people will take notice. But they often won't let that single incident permanently brand you. I remember a friend in the entertainment business who made an enormous bet, involving many millions of his company's dollars, on a project with a TV star. The project was a failure, and the company's entire investment went down the drain. The thinking among all who knew him was that our friend was doomed. His reputation would be forever tarnished by this colossal misstep. It didn't turn out that way. At first, people felt sorry for him. Then nostalgia took over; people started to joke about his epic bomb in the same way families a year or two later will laugh about a disastrous vacation that was anything but funny when they were going through it. Finally, and weirdly, his reputation actually got a favorable bounce from the whole episode. He came to be seen in the company as a daring swashbuckler, someone who wasn't afraid to swing for the fences while others chipped away for singles and doubles. Here was a fellow who was comfortable "playing in the big leagues." Before long, his catastrophe was perceived as a big bet that simply didn't work out. As I say, people can be very forgiving.

Paradoxically, people can be less generous after a one-time triumphal event. If you do something terrific early on—in your career or in a new job—people will certainly credit that to your emerging reputation. But they also want to wait and see if you can repeat the success. Anything less and they'll think your success was a fluke. This is how "one-hit-wonder" reputations are formed.

Repeat After Me

Reputations are formed by a sequence of actions that resemble one another. When other people see a pattern of resemblance, that's when they start forming *your* reputation.

For example, one day you're asked to make a presentation in a meeting. Speaking in public may be the greatest fear among adults, but in this instance you don't choke or crumble. You give a great presentation, magically emerging as someone who can stand up in front of people and be commanding, knowledgeable, and articulate. Everyone in attendance is impressed. They never knew this side of you. That said, this is not the moment when your reputation as a great public speaker jells into shape. But a seed has been sown in people's minds. If you repeat the performance another time, and another, and another, eventually your reputation as an effective speaker will solidify.

Negative reputations form in the same unhurried, incremental way. Let's say you're a fresh-faced manager looking at your first big crisis at work. You can react with poise or panic, clarity or confusion, aggressiveness or passivity. It's your call. In this instance, you do not distinguish yourself as a leader. You fumble the moment and your group takes the hit. Fortunately for you, this is not the moment when your reputation as someone who can't handle pressure is formed. It's too soon to tell. But again, the seed has been sown—and people are watching, waiting for a repeat performance. Only when you demonstrate your ineffectiveness in another crisis, and then another, will your reputation for wilting at crunch time take shape.

What's really puzzling about this is how little thought many of us give to the power of *repeat* behavior in our own actions. We're always on the lookout for it in others, scanning for patterns in how they respond to us, the way a poker player looks for an opponent's "tell." If you're a salesman, it's knowing, after many dealings with a customer, that the customer always buys if you drop a hint that someone else is interested. If you're a manager, it's knowing, after repeated crying sessions, that your assistant responds to your sarcasm with tears. If you're an assistant, it's knowing, after repeated blowups, not to bring a problem to the boss until he's had his morning coffee.

We're shrewd, alert, sometimes insightful in the mini-reputations we assign to the people we work with. But we rarely apply that insightfulness to ourselves. The customer who pants like a craving dog when he hears others are interested in the same deal probably doesn't know that about himself; if he did, he'd change his ways. Likewise, the boss who needs coffee to settle down at the start of day is probably in the dark about how his assistant is "managing" him.

Because we don't keep track of our repeat behavior, we never see the patterns that others see. These are the patterns that shape our reputation—and yet we're largely oblivious to them and, in turn, to our reputation.

You may feel an impulse to challenge this contention. But when was the last time you conducted your own behavioral review—and literally kept track of your "repeat performances," the good and the bad? If you had six occasions in the year when you came up with a universally acknowledged great idea in a meeting, have you analyzed those six moments to measure their impact on your reputation as a great "idea person"? Do you even know if you have that reputation, although you privately believe you deserve it?

In my experience, few if any of us do this sort of thing. We're too busy moving forward, dealing with immediate challenges, to look back for the patterns that are so obvious to others.

But all that changes now—with the following Reputation Questionnaire, which is designed to uncover patterns of repeat behavior in your career.

REPUTATION QUESTIONNAIRE

1. Name six "great" personal moments in the last twelve months at work. (You can consult your calendar, even ask family members—but not colleagues—to jog your memory.)

2. What made these moments "great"? (Give it your best shot. For example, was it an event that made you look good to others? Benefited your organization? Or was a learning experience for you?)

3. In what way, if any, did these moments resemble one another?

4. Can you identify the personal quality embodied in that resemblance? Can you give it a name? For example, if you cite two "great" moments when you went out of your way to help a colleague with advice, you would label that personal quality as "generosity"—which feeds into a reputation for being "generous."

5. On a scale of 1 to 10, with 10 being the most well known, how well known are these "great" moments to people you work with?

6. On a scale of 1 to 10, with 10 being the most agreement, how much would the people you work with agree with the personal qualities described in your answer to question #4?

7. Name six "bad" personal moments in the last twelve months.

8. What made these moments "bad"?

9. What did they have in common?

10. Can you identify the personal quality they had in common? Can you give it a name? For example, if two "bad" moments involve episodes where you lost your temper, the personal quality could be labeled as "hot-headed."

11. On a scale of 1 to 10, with 10 being the most well known, how well known are these "bad" moments to other people you work with?

12. On a scale of 1 to 10, with 10 being the most agreement, how much would the people you work with agree with the personal qualities described in your answer to question #10?

13. Which answer, to question #4 or #10, is most likely your current reputation? Or is it both?

I posed these questions to my friend, a financial manager named Patrick. Patrick's job is simple: to make money for his clients. And he is singularly devoted, even obsessed, with the responsibility he feels toward his clients. He has nightmares about losing a penny of their money. In other words, even without the daily metrics of client portfolios swinging up or down in value, Patrick is very aware of how he's performing.

For his "great" moments Patrick cited six examples of making money for clients, which he named "problem solving." His six "bad" moments revolved around not giving his clients all the attention he felt they deserved. He named this "missing in action." In question 13, he ranked "missing in action" more highly than "problem solving."

When I canvassed a dozen or so clients about Patrick, they universally praised his work and agreed that he was a "problem solver." In their minds, that was his reputation. They didn't care about or even acknowledge the problem he perceived of being "missing in action." In fact, they were quite happy with the attention they got. They felt it was just right, neither too much nor too little.

I realize this is a random, unscientific example, but I cite it as anecdotal evidence that even when things are going well for us—when, like Patrick, we're doing a good job and people recognize it—we may be clueless about our reputation. Perhaps like Patrick, who clearly worries too much and may start overcorrecting because of the responsibility he feels, we underestimate our great moments and overestimate the impact of our bad moments. Or perhaps we do the opposite.

Either way, that's what makes this questionnaire a useful tool. When you take it, it may be the first time you've ever spent time really thinking about the things you do that create a reputation. And if you get the people you work with to comment on your answers (which I recommend doing), you may be alarmed at the gap between how you see yourself and how others see you. But until you take this test and find out how others perceive you, you may never have a clue.

How to Change Your Reputation

I left out one final question from the questionnaire: *What are you going to do about it?* Here's where reputation gets tricky.

The truth is, reputation doesn't happen overnight. In the same way that *one event* can't form your reputation, *one corrective gesture* can't reform it either. You need a sequence of consistent, similar actions to begin the rebuilding process.

It's doable, but it requires personal insight and, most of all, discipline.

When I first start working one-on-one with clients to change their behavior, they want instant results. If their issue is, say, making sarcastic comments, they assume they can stop the sarcasm overnight and their colleagues will instantly applaud them for it. It doesn't work that way. I remind them that just as people's negative impression of them was formed over a period of months or years—time when they were delivering a steady diet of sarcasm—they'll need months of steady non-sarcastic behavior to undo that impression.

If you're known as a sarcastic boss, you have to bite your tongue *for a long time* for people to recognize the change and start accepting the new you. You can go for weeks without deviating, but just one incident where the old sarcastic you reappears and people may wonder if you've changed at all.

It's the same with any reputation. You have to be consistent in how you present yourself—to the point where you don't mind being "guilty of repeating yourself." If you abandon that consistency, people will get confused. The reputation you're trying to form gets muddied by conflicting evidence and eventually loses its sharp focus.

No one knows this better in our society than politicians. When they're campaigning for office, their primary goal is to pick a message and then repeat it ad nauseam to the electorate. That's what the political pros and strategists mean when they praise their candidate for "staying on message." It's the only way office-seekers can establish what they stand for and, by extension, their reputation. Reluctant as I am to cite any political tactic as an example of model behavior, I have to admit that being "on message" is one that I've come to respect. I tell my clients it's the easiest, most effective way to seize control of the impression you're trying to make—and maintain it.

Take a look around you at work. Who are the colleagues who have clear, positive reputations—and what are they doing to achieve this enviable position? You won't have to probe too deeply to see that an "on message" consistency is often their primary virtue. Without that consistency, we'd never see the pattern they're creating. Chances are that that consistency is not accidental. It's something they chose and articulated to themselves.

I used to marvel at an executive named Bill who rose to the highest ranks of his company and did it all within the hours of eight-thirty to five-thirty. He didn't work late, he didn't work weekends. He decided early on in his corporate career that his family was more important to him than work, so he set a personal goal of always being home by dinnertime—which meant that, despite being as ambitious as the next person, he had to get all his work done during regular work hours. He didn't have the cushion of working late or on weekends. And yet his results were excellent. He was liked and admired by everyone he worked with, which went some way to explaining his ascent at the company.

But it didn't explain everything.

"How did you do it?" I asked him.

"I always knew that my family came first," he said, "so I vowed that I wouldn't be one of those people who love trading office gossip or need to demonstrate that they're in the loop about all the company intrigue. If I could cut all that out of my workday—the small talk on the phone, the water-cooler distractions, the beer after work, the impromptu sessions to complain about senior management—I figured I'd save a lot of time each day. I could do my job and get home at a normal hour. And I pretty much kept my vow.

"It's funny though," he continued. "At first I was the company oddball. I was capable and got good performance reviews. People saw me as no fun, no frills, a late-model Ward Cleaver. The only thing missing was the cardigan. But I was consistent and steady, and over time, that sober persona became my signature—and a virtue. People started to think of me as someone who could be counted on like clockwork. I was 'dependable,' which is a reputation I'll take anytime. Because I didn't traffic in office small talk, my bosses grew to consider me as someone who could be trusted with confidential information—which is ironic: the less interested I was in other people's secrets, the more comfortable they were in sharing them with me. Eventually, my serious demeanor made people think I had leadership potential. People were willing to follow someone steady and dependable like me. I suppose they thought I wouldn't let them down. And once people are willing to follow you, the sky's the limit. All because I wanted to clock out at five-thirty."

Bill may be being modest. Whatever qualities others are responding to, one key to his success is his consistency. His repeat behavior gave people an unambiguous way of viewing him—which is what happens when you're disciplined about your objectives and follow through in your actions. After a while, people are locked into one way of interpreting your actions—because *you* have locked into it by choice—and your reputation falls neatly into place.

Another interesting fact about Bill: Even though his kids are grown and out of the house and he doesn't always have to leave work by five-thirty, he still sticks to his schedule. That's the best thing about creating a reputation for yourself: Do it right the first time and you may never have to change your ways.

By impacting our reputation we can impact our Mojo. Having a reputation that others find bothersome can make keeping your Mojo as easy as "pushing a big rock up a steep hill." It is theoretically possible, but practically challenging. Having a great reputation—in an area that matters in your life—makes Mojo maintenance more of a joy than a chore.

CHAPTER 7

Acceptance:
When Can You Let Go?

I have been a Buddhist for the last thirty-five years. I am not a religious Buddhist, I am a philosophical Buddhist. What I love about Buddhism is its psychology. This is a psychology that can be applied by anyone—no matter what your beliefs (or non-beliefs).

There is one area where Buddhism has given me an edge over many people I know. It has cured me of what I call the Great Western Disease.

The Great Western Disease afflicts anyone who says or thinks the phrase, "I'll be happy when . . ." And then fills in the blank.

I'll be happy when I have a million dollars in the bank.
I'll be happy when we can move to a bigger house.
I'll be happy when the kids graduate.
I'll be happy when I retire.
I'll be happy when I lose twenty pounds.
I'll be happy when the mortgage is paid off.

The list of ways we can fill in the blanks here is endless—as long as a listing of all human appetite and desire. But it's an illusion. When we get the million dollars, we're not satisfied; we want another million. When the kids are finally out of the house, we're not really "free"; some other responsibility—e.g., a sick parent—soon demands our attention. When we lose twenty pounds, the achievement is fleeting; we quickly learn that it's even tougher to keep the pounds off.

"I'll be happy when . . ." is a very Western way of thinking. We believe that *achieving* a goal will somehow make us happy, conveniently ignoring the fact that the goal line always moves slightly beyond our reach.

Sometimes we move it ourselves. There's nothing wrong with that. Without goals we would never achieve anything. The Great Western Disease is that we fixate on the future at the expense of enjoying the life we're living *now.*

That last thought is a hard concept for most people in the West to grasp because it requires the adoption of a non-Western mind-set and, in turn, the letting go of decades of Western (or cultural) programming.

I got a stark reminder of this not long ago when I was scheduled to meet my client Michael at my hotel in London. Michael was a chronically overscheduled executive who, in my experience, was fifteen minutes late to everything. As I looked out my room window a few minutes before our 10 A.M. appointment, I could see it was a beautiful spring morning—which made me reluctant to sit in my claustrophobic room waiting for Michael to ring me when he arrived. So I went down to the hotel lobby, sat down in a deep comfortable sofa, and waited.

The sun streamed in through the floor-to-ceiling lobby windows, providing a comforting touch of warmth on my skin. Through those windows, I could watch the parade of men and women rushing to work along the busy London street, an opportunity for people-gazing as compelling to me as a movie. I didn't have a care in the world. I wasn't thinking about what happened the day before. I wasn't thinking about upcoming events. I wasn't even thinking about Michael.

Michael eventually arrived—on cue, fifteen minutes late—speeding through the lobby toward me, offering the smooth, practiced, and profuse apologies the chronically tardy must utter several times a day. "I'm sorry for keeping you waiting, Marshall," he said. "You can't believe how busy traffic was at Trafalgar Square and . . ." I didn't hear the rest, because it didn't make any difference to me.

All he had done was interrupt my pleasant reverie in the lobby that morning. I wasn't annoyed that he was late. I was glad that he'd arrived. Since he was my client and we would be working closely together for many months, I wanted him to know that.

"Don't worry about it," I said. "I knew you'd show up. The only thing I didn't know was *when*. In the meantime, I had a nice time sitting here."

I'm usually not this pedantic, but seeing the confusion on his face, it occurred to me that Michael assumed that he had caused me distress by making me wait—because he would have been distressed if the tables had been turned. What he couldn't appreciate was that this is not how I think. It's not my mind-set.

In telling this story I'm not claiming a special level of enlightenment where I can greet any delay or disappointment with complete serenity. I am far from perfect (just ask my family) and I can get as upset over life's minor injustices as the next person. I differ from many people in one respect: When a perceived injustice happens and nothing can be done to turn back the clock, I do a pretty good job of just accepting it rather than whining and complaining about it. I can let it go. That's the meaning that should be taken from the episode in the London hotel lobby: Michael assumed that I was angry at him for his lateness; I had already accepted it and moved on.

I mention this example as a reminder that throughout this book you'll find that I'm fairly consistent about the concept of acceptance—especially in relation to how we deal with our past and future. It's not because I need to convert people to my way of thinking. It's because worrying about the past and being anxious about the future can easily destroy our Mojo. It upsets us emotionally. It clouds our judgment. It fills us with regret. And it can lead to self-punishment. This sort of thinking afflicts the high and the low, the rich and the poor, the achievers and the struggling.

For example, on a flight from Zurich to New York, I found myself sitting next to a wealthy investor who had discovered that he'd paid too much for a small high-tech firm. I knew this because he couldn't stop talking about it. He was livid with the founder of the company, who he felt had misled him in the sale. Breakthrough technologies that were promised never materialized. Revenue targets were consistently missed. Deals in negotiation always fell through. The founder himself, after making a powerful initial impression, turned out to be somewhat of a slacker, who lacked motivation and consistently missed business commitments.

I asked my seatmate how long this guy had been upsetting him. "Months," he said, gritting his teeth.

This wasn't the first time I had seen behavior like this. We all know someone whose behavior drives us crazy, frustrates us, or makes us feel guilty or sad. We've all spent hours reliving how someone was inconsiderate or ungrateful or less than straightforward. Just thinking about that person jacks up our pulse.

It also wasn't the first time I had seen this behavior in someone who "has it all" and should be able to put an annoying individual behind him. My seatmate was a multimillionaire, with a beautiful home and family in Switzerland. He had investments in several standout companies. All these positives should easily have canceled out this one nettlesome person in his life. He should have been happy on that plane, but instead he was making himself miserable.

I suggested that maybe he wasn't as angry at the founder as he was at himself—for being a poor judge of character and not conducting adequate due diligence in the purchase.

He admitted the possibility, then began berating himself. "I usually have a great instinct for these deals. How did I screw this up?"

This wasn't the progress I'd been hoping for. He had just taken two steps forward and one step back. He was now angry with himself for the mistake, which was just as fruitless as raging about the slacker founder.

I went on to remind him that despite this one mistake he was still very successful. I suggested that he write off this one bad deal as a learning experience that he could apply to his next acquisition. But I wasn't sure that would assuage the anger he felt at himself and the other guy. He not only had to accept the situation, he had to forgive both of the people involved.

"Let me ask you something," I said. "I can see this guy really gets under your skin. How much sleep do you think this person is losing over *you* right now?"

"None," he groaned.

"So who is being punished here?" I asked. "And who is doing the punishing?"

"That would be me—twice," he said.

That's when the message got through to him. Angry as he was, he was also practical. He wanted to stop being consumed by anger. Acceptance (and its follow-up, forgiveness) was a direct way to do that.

"What do you suggest?" he asked.

"Well, I'd either fire the founder or sell the company. But before that, I'd work on forgiving myself."

It took a big chunk of the flight, but eventually he understood.

When we cannot accept a situation for what it is and we refuse to forgive people for causing that situation, who do we ultimately hurt? The answer is always the same: ourselves. By carrying around anger and negative baggage, we weigh ourselves down. We limit our opportunities to find meaning and happiness. We kill our Mojo.

That's what makes acceptance—warm and fuzzy as it may sound to Western minds—as important as identity, achievement, and reputation in building our Mojo. It's the element that liberates us from toxic emotions. When everything around us seems confusing, acceptance reminds us what really matters.

Try it the next time you find yourself engorged with anger at someone who has disappointed or hurt you. Ask yourself who is making *you* feel upset, angry, or crazy. Then set aside every thought, every argument, every image about the people who are upsetting you. Blank all of it out—and focus on these people as they are in your life now. Not on what they did in the past. Not on what you want to happen to them in the future. Getting upset with other people for being who they are makes as much sense as kicking a chair for being a chair. Your chair cannot help but be a chair. Neither can the people who upset you. They're being who they are. (If you had their parents, their genes, their résumé, you might be them too.) You don't have to like them, agree with them, or even respect them. Just accept them for being who they are.

When you can do that, you can forgive them for being who they are—and forgive yourself for being who you are.

Like my seatmate from Zurich, you have just taken a most important step in regaining your Mojo.

By focusing on acceptance, I am, in no way, suggesting that you should not try to create change—and try to make the world a better place. I am just suggesting that you should change what you can and "let go" of what you cannot change.

CHAPTER 8

Mojo Killers

What kills Mojo in a career?

Missing the big opportunity
Getting passed over for a promotion
Getting demoted
Losing a lot of money
Getting fired
Going bankrupt

You know the list. It's our worst nightmare come true. These are the screaming headlines and public humiliations that suck all the spirit and forward thrust from our professional lives and surround us with a negative don't-come-near-me aura, as if we were walking Hazmat zones.

But these humbling episodes are results, not causes. They're what the scoreboard says at the end of the game, not during the game itself. They don't reveal what happened; they only reveal the consequences of our actions and choices. When people go from Mojo to Nojo, it's usually because of a series of simple, hard-to-spot mistakes that lead up to the humiliating result—mistakes like these:

1. Over-Committing

There's a wise saying, "If you want to get something done, ask a busy person." It makes sense up to a point. A busy person is demonstrably well organized and not inclined to waste time or get distracted by nonessential issues. A busy person is practiced at the art of going from A to B to C, skipping D and E, and eventually delivering results. But there's a fine line between taking on a lot of work and taking on too much.

It's easy to see how people in corporate situations fall into this over-commitment trap. If you're good at what you do and like your job—i.e., you're bursting with Mojo—everybody wants to rub up against you in some way. They want you in their meeting. They seek out your opinion of an idea. They ask you to run a project for them. People with high Mojo tend to be assaulted with opportunities. This happens at all levels, high and low. It's how junior employees advance more rapidly than their peers; their enthusiasm and ambition tempt bosses to pile on the work until the employees cry uncle, which they never do ("I can't handle it" is the last thing a young ambitious person wants to admit)—until it's too late. That's when the quality of their work—and their Mojo—begins to falter in a predictable but vicious circle.

It's even easier to see how self-employed people fall hard for this. When you don't have the cushion of a steady paycheck, every opportunity looks like your last payday. And in a faltering economy, that wolf-at-the-door feeling is even more intense. So you say yes to everything.

I'm also guilty of this. For example, when I speak to groups, I work for myself in what could simply be regarded as "day labor." I show up and share what I know—and like any wage earner, I get paid for my time. Thus, when someone invites me to talk to them or their organization, it's a straightforward pay-for-work opportunity for me. If I show up, I get paid. If I say, "No, thanks," I'm tossing money down the drain. I deal with this by filling up my schedule with bookings months in advance, which tells me where the quiet periods are in my calendar. I regard these periods of unbooked days as valuable time reserved for reading or writing or simply chilling out.

But then temptation appears. Someone calls up to hire me. I say I can't do it. But they persist. They'll work around my schedule, which is the first step in wearing down my already fragile resistance. There's also the element of flattery at work against me too. These nice people are telling me, "We want you!"—and they'll take me on my terms. You have to be more hard-hearted than I am to say no to folks like that. Plus, the date in question is several months away. Who knows what the economy or my future bookings will look like then? So I switch from "Can't make it" to "I'm there for you." And that's how I find myself on the road, unpacking my suitcase in another hotel, preparing to get up on a nice Saturday morning in May or June to talk to a roomful of clients—when I might be better served writing my next book.

I'm not whining. I know I'm lucky and that I'm describing a high-class headache that most people in my line of work would jump at. I'm also not saying that the fine people who hire me under these circumstances get any less of my enthusiasm. But the simple fact that I question my decision to accept the booking represents a threat to my Mojo. It injects the potential for regret into the experience—and it's just possible that a tiny drop of that emotion may bleed into my performance. If during the year I say yes too many times when I should be saying no, that feeling could compound to dangerous levels—and turn into burnout. Although I'm the guy writing this book, I still have a lot to learn about avoiding over-commitment! How about you?

If we chronically over-commit, our sagging spirit inside may well become manifestly obvious to everyone. Our formerly enjoyable job can become rote, our execution sloppy and halfhearted. The irony of all this—that our habit of over-committing (in time) has produced the unintended consequence of making us appear under-committed (in spirit)—is rarely appreciated by our customers or our colleagues.

We all feel over-committed on occasion. We can all benefit by realizing that we can fall into this trap. You rarely hear people say, "I'm taking on too much work"—although we all can see that most of us are working longer and harder hours than ever in today's 24/7 economy. Perhaps they're afraid of looking weak, as if they can't handle any challenge that comes their way. Perhaps they can't resist the siren call of being asked to help out; it's a validation of their skill and another way of being told, "We love you." Perhaps with all their Mojo they really do believe they have superhuman qualities and that nothing is too much. Perhaps they realize that "I took on too much" is not much of an excuse if and when they drop the ball (after all, it was their choice to say yes or no).

Any one of these reasons explains why over-committing is one of the sweet but risky blowbacks from having Mojo—and why it's a stealth Mojo killer.

Before replying with an enthusiastic "yes" to that next request, think of the long-term impact on your Mojo. Are you doing what is right for the long-term? Or just saying what make others happy in the short-term? Is what you are about to commit to going to increase the long-term happiness and meaning that you experience in life?

2. Waiting for the Facts to Change

In early 2009 I was talking with a lawyer named Tom about the bankruptcy of the 360-attorney law firm where he had been vice-chairman. It was a 120-year-old firm that specialized in a narrow segment of securities law that had vanished overnight with the financial meltdown the year before. As one of the firm's leaders, Tom was besieged by his now-jobless attorneys for advice on what to do. Few if any of them had ever in their lives experienced such a setback—and they were more than a little lost.

I was eager to know what sage advice Tom shared with them, but instead he told me a story about his first year in law school.

"A big part of our training as lawyers," Tom said, "was to interpret a pattern of facts so that we could advise a client. Our teacher would give us a hypothetical set of facts and then go around the classroom asking, "What would you do?" Every student would respond with a course of action. The answers weren't always correct or even reasonably intelligent. Sometimes they were desperate. But the students always came up with some rationale, some idea to act on. At no point in these classroom exercises did any of my classmates say, 'I'm going to wait until the situation changes.'

"And yet," Tom continued, "that's what a lot of my highly educated attorneys—and, I suspect, millions of other people facing similar setbacks—are doing. They're looking around and telling themselves, 'I'll be okay when the economy improves.'"

"In other words," I said, "they're doing the opposite of what they were trained to do in law school."

"That's right," Tom said. "They're waiting for the facts to change back to something they can understand, something more palatable. They're refusing to accept that the situation has already changed dramatically—and it's unlikely that things will go back to the way they were. It's just not the way history works. They're denying the evidence right in front of them."

"So, what did you say to the young attorneys?" I asked.

"I gave them a verbal cold shower. I said, 'The firm we worked at is not coming back. It got buried by a rotten economy, but it's not magically resurrecting when the economy revives. Something else might take its place. But neither you nor I can say what that is. You can't sit around waiting for the situation to change. You have to come up with a course of action, just like we all did in law school. Find another area of the law. Hang up your own shingle. Transfer your legal skills to another business. But don't wait for a new career to come to you.'"

Waiting for the facts to change—instead of dealing with the facts as they are—is a common response to a setback. It's the response of the owner of a dying business who refuses to cut costs or lay off workers during a continued downturn because a turnaround is just around the corner. It's the response of a shopkeeper in a decaying part of town who gamely sticks to his product line and his way of doing business even as customers disappear, revenue shrinks, and neighboring stores shut down. The area will come back, he thinks; it can't simply vanish.

When people wait for discomfiting facts to change into something more to their liking, they're basically engaging in wishful thinking. It's the opposite of over-committing because it leads to under-acting (or under-committing and not acting at all). Instead of doing something, you're frozen in place while you wait for a more comforting set of facts to appear. In a world that's constantly rushing forward, this is akin to moving backward. That's a Mojo killer.

When the facts are not to your liking, ask yourself, "What path would I take if I knew that the situation would not get better?" Then get ready to do that. If the world changes in your favor, you haven't lost anything. If the facts do not change, you are more ready to face the new world.

3. Looking for Logic in All the Wrong Places

I think we can all agree that the world is not a particularly rational place. Humans are not logical. If we were, wars would never begin and people wouldn't buy overpriced homes with no money down and loans they could never repay.

Humans, in fact, are profoundly illogical. Yet we devote many of our waking hours to trying to find logic in situations where no logic exists.

Our minds need order and fairness and equity and justice. But much of life is neither fair nor just. That's a problem for many of us—and a Mojo killer.

If I had to pick educational backgrounds that breed employees who excessively "look for logic," I would nominate engineers, scientists, computer programmers, and math majors. (I was a math major and went to an undergraduate engineering school, so I know a little about which I speak). Once we "logical thinkers" make peace with the fact that all decisions are made by real people—not logical computers—life gets easier, we make more of a positive difference, and we are happier. That's just the way it works.

Another place our need to be logical can quickly kill our Mojo is at home. Many of us, as spouses and partners, lose Mojo at home because of our persistent need to use our logic to prove that our partners are wrong in pointless arguments. This is so common that ministers frequently remind newly married couples to ask themselves, "Would you rather be right—or have a happy marriage?"

Sometimes, we hope that logic will prevail against all odds to reveal to all that we are in the right, and we stick to our guns—until the bitter, bitter end. This happened some years ago to a friend of mine named Tim who was working as a producer at a cable channel. Tim was in charge of all evening programming—and felt he was on track to run the channel someday. Then the corporate parent installed a woman from headquarters as Tim's boss. She had no experience in broadcasting, but she was very adept at impressing her superiors, providing good quotes to the media, and shaping her executive persona.

Tim hated her immediately. He fought with her and complained about her incessantly to colleagues, making no effort to mask his contempt for her. Tim believed that in a logical world, her shallowness would be exposed and his brilliance rewarded. Tim thought that his superior broadcasting expertise was a powerful shield, more powerful than the woman's power to fire him anytime she wanted. He didn't count on running out of time. Within a year, the woman got fed up with Tim's belligerence and sent him packing. A year later, her ineptitude caught up with her and she was given the boot too. Tim might have been right about her, but that was small consolation. He had lost his job—and his Mojo—in his hope that "logic" would prevail.

Remember our friend Tim the next time your need to be "logical" overcomes your common sense.

If you're looking for your own view of logic to win the day, you may be looking in the wrong place. If you focus on making a positive difference, instead of just being satisfied with feeling "objective," you will benefit both your company and your career. You may ultimately increase, rather than damage, your Mojo.

The next time you pride yourself on your superior "logic" and damage relationships with the people you need at work—or the people you love at home—ask yourself, "How logical was that?"

4. Bashing the Boss

A company named DDI did some fascinating research that showed that the average American spends fifteen hours a month criticizing or complaining about their boss. Since I didn't do this research myself, and let my own ego get in the way, I chose to believe that they were wrong. When I conducted a similar study of two hundred employees, my results were exactly the same as theirs. They were right!

Many of us bash the boss at work, after work, even on weekends when our only audiences are our partners or captive family members. That fifteen hours is more time than Americans devote to watching baseball, which suggests that our real national pastime is bashing the boss.

A little bit of boss bashing may be understandable, in the same way that stepping outside to scream at the top of our lungs releases some of our pent-up frustrations. But whatever therapeutic benefit we derive from this form of complaining is far outweighed by the negatives.

For one thing, it's not particularly attractive. Trashing the boss when he or she is not in the room to put up a defense makes even the most eloquent whiner appear small and cowardly. People wonder why you don't say it to the boss's face. They may also wonder what you are saying about them out of earshot.

It's futile to critique people who aren't even in the room. They can't hear you talking or respond to what you are saying (although trust me, through boss's intuition, he or she senses your disdain). Nothing constructive will come out of it. You won't build a better boss with your jibes. You'll only tarnish your reputation and lower your Mojo.

More than anything, boss bashing is unproductive. Imagine what you could accomplish if you dedicated those fifteen hours to something of consequence (like going to night school or being with your family, the way Bill did in Chapter 6)?

Combine those negatives, plus the risk that the boss may hear about you through office gossip (or overhear you when you think no one's listening), and you have built the perfect mechanism for turning the positive spirit you feel about what you're doing into a negative spirit both inside and out. It's the definition of a Mojo killer.

The next time you start to bash the boss, think about what you may be doing to your own Mojo and the Mojo of the people around you. If you really have a problem with bosses, *talk to them* about it. If you feel that you cannot talk with them, leave. If you cannot talk with them, and cannot leave, revisit our chapter on "acceptance" and make the best of it.

5. Refusing to Change Because of "Sunk Costs"

A sunk cost is a cost that cannot be recovered once incurred. It's a well-studied concept in economics and game theory, explaining why we make irrational decisions against our best interests. But the concept rears its head in many of our daily decisions, big and small.

Let's say you buy two $100 tickets to a Broadway play two months in advance for you and your husband. The play is a star vehicle for your favorite actress, whom you've never seen live onstage. That's the only reason you're going. A couple of days before the performance you learn that the star is ill and will be replaced by an understudy, who has received terrible reviews, the night you're attending. What do you do? Your husband is neutral; he'll do whatever you decide. Do you write off the $200 in tickets, figuring you have no interest in suffering through the play without the star? Or do you go anyway, reluctant to throw away the tickets—your sunk cost—justifying the additional costs of getting to the theater and dining in Manhattan by convincing yourself that the understudy might get better.

An economist would immediately point out that the "smarter" decision is to stay home. Either way, the $200 has been spent and cannot be recovered, so why worry about it or build around it decisions that will cost you additional money—and probably make you frustrated? But of course, many of us can't block out the sunk cost; it becomes the benchmark of value against which all other choices are made. It's not rational, but it's real.

I started paying attention to people's foolish devotion to sunk costs in the early 1980s when I read historian Barbara Tuchman's *The March of Folly*, her superb study of the pervasive presence of what she calls "mental standstill" in governments. Here's how she described it:

> In its first stage mental standstill fixes the principles and boundaries governing a political problem. In the second stage, when dissonances and failing function begin to appear, the initial principles rigidify. This is the period when, if wisdom were operative, re-examination and rethinking and a change of course are possible, but they are as rare as rubies in a backyard. Rigidifying leads to increase of investment and the need to protect egos; policy founded upon error multiplies, never retreats. The greater the investment and the more involved in it the sponsor's ego, the more unacceptable is disengagement.

Tuchman was explaining great historic moments of folly, such as Britain's loss of America and the U.S. humiliation in Vietnam. She concluded that "to recognize error, to cut losses, to alter course, is the most repugnant option in government." She may as well have been talking about all of us, not just governments and leaders.

Her concept explains why when an investment loses half its value, rather than cut our losses and get out *now,* we hang on until the investment is worth practically nothing. We persist in error because we cannot admit error.

Tuchman's book opened my eyes to the many forms of "standstill"—not only mental, but emotional and professional—around me. When my UCLA colleagues would respond defensively, even violently, to well-meaning constructive criticism of their research papers, I saw it as another sign of the "sunk cost" fallacy. They were so attached to their years of hard researching and writing that they couldn't brook an alternative viewpoint. It was the same when I heard people making excuses for their poor behavior. After living with their dysfunctional behavior for so many years (a sunk cost if there ever was one), people become invested in defending their dysfunctions rather than changing them.

Sometimes even achieving a desired level of success can be a sunk cost that limits your Mojo. I learned this from my mentor, Paul Hersey. I was thirty years old at the time. I had a Ph.D. in Organizational Behavior and I had fashioned a nice professional life as an expert on customized 360-degree feedback programs and their implementation. My modus operandi wasn't complicated. Companies would hire me to study their operations and tailor a "three-sixty" just for them. That was a large part of what I did. We then designed training and follow-up around these inventory results. It was a very narrow specialty, but I'd sort of invented it, so I could charge a healthy day rate for my time. To a poor boy from Kentucky who had just spent eight prime years as a penniless grad student, any paycheck would have been a wild success—and I was doing better than that.

Then Paul Hersey took me aside and said, "Marshall, your problem is you're making too much money. You're very successful running around selling days and getting paid. But you're becoming addicted to this success. At your current pace, all you'll ever do is run around and sell your days. You'll have a good life, but you'll never be what you could be."

Dr. Hersey made me see that what I considered success had locked me, happily and obliviously, in place. I didn't have the vision or guts to shake up my reliable way of making a living and expand my horizons. That would mean taking a risk. It would mean jettisoning some of what I had invested in developing my customized 360s—my "sunk cost"—and turning to something else. I'm convinced that if Paul hadn't pointed this out, I'd still be doing today what I was doing at thirty. (By the way, the economic value of doing this has rapidly declined because of the Internet—so even my financial benefits would have eroded.)

After finally listening to Paul's advice, I began writing and doing research that had no short-term financial reward, but produced huge long-term career benefits. The positive difference in my long-term Mojo was huge!

We all have sunk costs in our lives—because if we're remotely successful it wasn't all by luck. We had to invest a big piece of ourselves in our work. That "investment" may have stopped paying off without us being aware of it.

Take a look around you. Are your decisions based on what you might lose or what you have to gain? If it's the former, your devotion to sunk costs might be costing you more than you know. It may cost you your Mojo.

6. Confusing the Mode You're In

Successful people operate in two modes: professional and relaxed.

In professional mode, we're at our image-conscious best. We pay attention to what we say, how we look, whom we must serve, and whom we can't afford to displease. In relaxed mode, we're less guarded. We're grilling in the backyard rather than eating in the corporate dining room. We're riding a motorcycle rather than driving a sedan. It's the difference between who we are on weekends and who we are on weekdays.

Our Mojo is at risk when we shift from professional to relaxed mode without making everyone aware of the shift—probably because we're not aware of it ourselves.

I was once asked to work with a client who had this problem. She was a senior executive at a large retail chain, with all the attributes to succeed the current CEO: dedicated, hardworking, got results, looked professional, acted like a leader, and cared about people. She was the total package except for one thing: Get a couple of drinks under her belt while she was hanging out with her "peeps," whether in the bar near the office at the end of the day or on the corporate jet on the way to a meeting, and she would start blasting her coworkers with funny, cynical remarks. She spared no one from her sarcastic commentary.

It wasn't the alcohol, I concluded. It was the situation. Nor was it an occasional lapse, like an episode of inappropriate behavior at the company Christmas party. There was a pattern here. She would be the perfect high-Mojo executive all day, but after most of the employees had gone home, she'd call her friends into her office, let down her guard, and demonstrate her humorous cynicism. Now, there's nothing wrong with cynicism. In an absurd, irrational world like ours, we'd be nuts if we didn't harbor some dark, funny thoughts about other people. But most of us keep them to ourselves, or express them with extreme selectivity.

It was a sign of the CEO's faith in this executive that when he found out about this behavior (he had received some complaints), he hired me to help this person change. The first thing I told the executive was "This is really stupid behavior. Please don't do this again."

She reflected upon what she had done and soberly agreed. "You are right. In hindsight, this is really stupid. Don't worry, it won't happen again."

Then we went through what triggered this behavior, so she could avoid it in the future. That's when we identified the contrast in her life between relaxed and professional mode. What happened was pretty basic: She'd get in a room with her loyal subordinates after work and assume that anything she said was "just between us friends," as if they were all within a circle of trust. It never occurred to her that such trust could be broken, that one of her buddies would tell a coworker. "This is just between friends, you'll never believe what the boss said about . . ." And so on to another person, and another. Pretty soon everyone in the company knew what she had said. Even worse, when the stories were retold, the sarcastic humor was sometimes lost—and she just came off as angry—not funny.

In professional mode, she almost never made mistakes. In relaxed mode, her judgment weakened. She didn't appreciate that the higher up you are, the bigger the megaphone. No one would care if the doorman at headquarters talked this way. But when you're in a leadership position, everything you say is gossip fodder. And you can't control that.

Nor did she appreciate that she was giving a seal of approval to her employees to mimic her behavior. After all, the people below her weren't doing anything worse than she was.

I don't usually put much stock in *why* people do stupid things. I'm only interested in getting them to stop doing them. But in this case, I thought the cause was revealing: I think she turned sarcastic in relaxed mode because it made people laugh and, in turn, made her look clever and funny (see our need to appear smart in Chapter 6). She is a wonderful person with a good heart. She had no bad intent and did not want to hurt anyone. She just thought she was being "funny."

Helping this executive change was easy. All I had to do was help her see that in professional mode, she almost never made mistakes. In relaxed mode, she almost always made mistakes. So I told her, "Avoid operating in relaxed mode. Assume that people are always paying attention and that you, a top executive, need to be a consistent role model as a leader." I reminded her that a lot of people assume that the professional you is somehow "unreal," that the "real" you appears when you let your guard down. Ultimately, her behavior had to put a dent in her Mojo—because of the garbled signals she was sending about what she felt inside as opposed to what she was showing on the outside. If she was ever going to be a truly great leader, she would have to close the gap between her professional and relaxed selves, if only to eliminate the confusion over which one was really her.

That hit home. A woman who was the consummate professional for so much of her day found it anathema that people thought she was not being genuine all the time.

Her problem was never in her "heart"; her problem was in her "delivery." When she was "relaxed," she crossed the line from funny to unprofessional.

I suspect all of us could step back and analyze how often we drift out of professional mode into relaxed mode at work. Some of us do it fluidly, so no one notices the difference. Some of us do it abruptly and without warning, so that the differences are unsettling to our coworkers. If you look around your company, you'll see that the executives you most admire tend to be those who, with consistent discipline, never drift out of professional mode. It's not that they can't crack a joke or laugh at themselves or kick back at the end of the day. They're not grim grinds. But they have clear ideas about their identity, achievement, and reputation. They have chosen a role for themselves, and they rarely go off script. They are professionals. That's why they have Mojo.

But the Mojo Killers that we have discussed so far are not the only mental lapses that affect our positive spirit. There's one more that's so universal it deserves a chapter all by itself. It's about pointless arguments.

CHAPTER 9

Four Pointless Arguments

In many cases, our Mojo is at risk because of forces beyond our control. The economy sours. A big customer stops buying. A new competitor takes away market share. Our company has a bad quarter. And, assuming we still have a job after such setbacks, we feel the brunt of it in the form of heightened pressure and insecurity at work. If we lose our job, our Mojo may suffer. If we keep our job, our Mojo may still suffer.

Unlike the global economy, our proclivity to get into pointless arguments is something that we can control. Arguing can put our Mojo at risk by needlessly creating enemies that could have been allies. I say "needlessly" because many of our arguments fall into classic patterns that, if looked at from a distance, would seem silly and beneath our dignity. We don't have to do this. We can engage if we choose—or we can abstain—as the situation warrants.

I completely agree that it is worth arguing over true injustice in the workplace or in the world. What I am discussing here is arguing about perceived injustices that usually say more about our own egos than the "cause" that we are championing.

By recognizing classic argument traps, we can better determine which battles to fight—and which battles to avoid. At work, and even more so at home, even the arguments that we "win" can be Pyrrhic victories that are not worth the cost of engagement.

1. Let Me Keep Talking

Everyone, at work or at home, has opinions. And the vast majority of human beings enjoy expressing these opinions. In fact, we like to see this as our right. The arguments begin when people feel they're not getting the chance to be heard—when someone tells them, in effect, "Be quiet already."

Sometimes we just go too far. Sometimes we just can't stop. Sometimes the final-decision-makers have heard all they are going to hear and believe that it is time to "move on." It can be very hard for smart, committed people—especially stubborn people—to just "let it go."

"Be quiet already" comes in many guises, running the range from obnoxious (someone actually saying "Shut up!") to euphemistic ("I appreciate your input"). In between are a variety of thoughtful or thoughtless tactics that aim to silence us. These include the decision-maker cutting you off in mid-sentence and asking, "Anything else on your mind?" Or saying, "I got it. Next." Or a colleague rolling his eyes while you're talking. Or interrupting to change the subject. No matter how well disguised the tactic, the net result is the same. We've lost the argument.

Rather than just admitting that we tried to sell our point and did not succeed, we may find decision-makers' efforts to stop us from continuing as insulting! We are so convinced that we are right, we believe that if we keep talking, just a little more, they will "see the light" and change their minds.

That's the moment when many people ratchet up—rather than tone down—their campaign to be heard (or in this case, re-heard). People who've lost the argument may search for a new way to revive the debate, usually by picking a fight over it with the person who rejected their input. What they don't realize, of course, is that it was over—the moment they were silenced and the initial discussion turned to another subject. Trying to revisit the subject hours, days, or weeks later, is like being a debater who missed the opportunity to make a lethal point early in the debate— and tries to make up for it by introducing "What I should have said" at a later point, long after everyone has moved on.

When we think we're not being heard, we tend to shout even louder— which is about the time others cover their ears or run out of the room.

One of my favorite clients has a great slogan called "Challenge up and support down." This company encourages every employee to express their opinion. It encourages every manager to listen. It also recognizes that there is a time and place to end the argument, to shake hands and move on as a team.

When we keep "fighting after the bell has rung," we can start damaging our reputation and, ultimately, our Mojo. In the end we will not win more arguments, we will win less. Our arguing will be viewed more as our own stubborn need to prove we are right than as a sincere commitment to help our organization.

2. I Had It Rougher Than You

I have always taken some foolish pride in the humble nature of my upbringing. For lots of us, it's part of being an American: reveling in how poor we were and how much we had to overcome in order to achieve our current station in life. Since Horatio Alger, this has been part of the "American Dream." It's the reason parents still lecture their children with memories of *their* childhoods that begin with "When I was your age . . ." There's nothing wrong with a little of that if the lecture imparts some useful instruction—and the children aren't rolling their eyes thinking, *Dad's at it again.* In general, this is a waste of time.

While "I had it so tough!" is bad at home, it can be even worse at work. When we do this, all we're doing is trying to elicit other people's admiration for our having had it rougher than they did. It's pointless, almost perverse bragging—and what does the "winner" of the argument really win? I embarrassed myself when I got into a contest with a client about which one of us was poorer growing up. After laying out all the necessities of modern life that we lacked in Valley Station, I tossed down my trump card: "The first three years in grade school," I said, "we had an outhouse."

My adversary countered, "In West Virginia, all we had were outhouses. What's the big deal? And by the way, we had dirt floors in my home!"

"You know what?" I said. "You win. I can't top dirt floors."

I felt like a fool afterward. And I suspect that the winner didn't feel any better. That's what happens when you try to glorify your past for all its deficiencies and all the suffering it brought upon you. It's no different for any debate about details in the past, even the good times. All you're doing is creating a contest of competing memories. Except for its limited self-entertainment value, what's the point of that?

3. Why Did You Do That?

This is a perennially pointless argument—because we never really know what other people's motives are for doing something that affects us. We can speculate—with generosity, if we attribute goodwill to their motives; or with paranoia, if we suspect hostile intent—but no matter how strenuously we probe, we may never get a completely frank answer. Leaders have gone to war for centuries without revealing their true motive for spending so much of their nation's blood and treasure. And so it is in the workplace: People do things that annoy or enrage us, and it's almost impossible to get to the bottom of why they did them, yet we waste hours trying.

This is not cynicism. Think about the last time someone questioned your motives. Did you respond with concern—or just get angry and feel like arguing?

Remember this when you find yourself angrily asking, "Why did you do that?" In almost all cases, negative attributions are met with hostility. Since you can never "prove" the other person had ill intent, you can never really "win" this pointless argument. If the other person did truly have bad intent, they would never admit it in a public debate. If the other person did not have bad intent, they will be hurt by your unfair comments. What have you won in either attempted argument? Nothing. What have you lost? Mojo.

4. It's Not Fair

A reporter at the *Chicago Tribune* once asked me if managers today are more abusive than in the past (a logical question in a discussion of executive behavior).

"Are you kidding me?" I said. "Not so long ago we fought a civil war because half of America thought slavery was a good thing. If that isn't abusive, what is? We used to have sweatshops. As recently as thirty years ago in the U.S. a manager could pretty much say anything to an employee and get away with it."

We've come a long way. Most major companies now believe in certain "inalienable rights" at work. We have the right to be treated with respect. We have the right to be judged by our performance and character rather than by a fluke of lucky birth. If we're women, we have the right to be paid as much as a man for doing the same job. When inequities such as these arise, they're worth arguing over.

But a lot of small stuff remains. A colleague gets a promotion we thought we deserved. The boss showers a rival division with money, ignoring our area. We're given a hiring freeze while others get every new person they ask for. This is the stuff that still makes us howl, "It's not fair!" (as if we are children again, complaining that a younger sibling got a better birthday gift than we received at the same age).

Such "equity" moments resemble one another in one clear way: A decision has been made that we disagree with. What's worse, we believe that we are not getting a good explanation—although that doesn't stop us from re-asking, which is the same as arguing over it. And when we do get another explanation, it's not good enough for us.

Let's say you've made it as one of three finalists competing for a job. All three of you are qualified, presentable, likeable, and skilled enough to jump through the employer's job-search hoops. That's why you're finalists; you're basically equal. You know that two of you will be disappointed—because only one person can win. What's upsetting to most people is the endgame of this scenario. When all things are equal, the differentiating reasons get sliced thinner and thinner, until they can seem flaky to us (i.e., not fair). We may believe thet we were not chosen because our mother didn't go to the same high school as the boss. Maybe we think it's because we don't share a passion with the boss for the same baseball team. Maybe we assume it is because we look younger than we really are. Whatever the reasons we are given, they will not satisfy us. Decision-makers make decisions. It doesn't mean they are right, or fair, or deeply care about our feelings. It only means that some other person decides—and we don't. Arguing that inequity won't change the outcome. It will only make us sound like peevish children.

Great influencers are like great salespeople. When the customers don't buy, they don't whine and blame the customers. They focus on what they can learn and do a better job next time. Great influencers keep their Mojo. Poor influencers lose it.

These four "losing" arguments all have the same end result. We don't change the outcome. We don't help our organizations or our families. We don't help ourselves. We only lower our Mojo.

CHAPTER 10

That Job Is Gone!

On a trip back home in 2008 I had lunch with an old friend, Joanie. She talked about the differences between the life her father, Bob, had and the one her son, Jared, was having.

"My dad didn't really like to work," she said. "He always put in the minimum number of hours, called in sick whenever possible, and did just enough to keep his job. He worked in a manufacturing job and, like all the hourly employees, he was protected by the union. He had no special training or education. He never went to an 'adult education' course in his life. He didn't have to. Once he was hired, he assumed that he had the job until he retired. And he was right.

"In hindsight, even though he didn't care much for his job, Dad had a pretty easy life. We lived in a small but nice home in a safe neighborhood in the suburbs. We had a big yard, where my mother had her own vegetable garden. Mom didn't need to have a job outside the home. Dad started working fresh out of high school and he was able to retire in his early fifties. He had a great pension and a health-care plan that took care of him and my mom for more than thirty years after he stopped working. The two of them traveled all around the country, went to Florida every winter, and never worried about money."

Joanie's voice changed as she talked about the life her son, Jared, was confronting.

"Jared has three years of college and works as much overtime as he can at a huge distribution center outside of town. He's twenty-six years old and still lives at home. He doesn't have a union protecting him. He doesn't have a pension plan, and the health plan is decent, not great. The way it looks now, Jared's chances of having the same home, security, and benefits that my dad took for granted are slim, even if he gets married and he and his wife both work."

For a moment there I actually thought I saw Joanie misting up with nostalgia about the life her father had—which is pretty ironic considering that her father worked for thirty-five years at a job he didn't really care about. He showed up at work, collected a paycheck, and practically counted the days until he could retire. (As it turned out, he lived a long life and took out far more pension and health benefits than he ever put in.)

The financial elements of her father's life were what she wished for her son, Jared. She wanted him to be able to buy a house like his grand-father's, work forty hours a week, take four weeks of vacation a year, and have lifetime health-care and pension benefits. To Jared this wouldn't be a curse. He'd be grateful for such a life. To Jared such a life would be suc-ceeding.

Here's the problem: Those jobs don't exist anymore.* They've been exported beyond our borders (without the same salaries, security, and benefits). And even if the jobs have stayed inside the U.S., many of the long-term benefits that made them so attractive have been stripped out by the forces of cost-cutting and global competition. What's even harder to accept is that those jobs are not coming back.

If I could write a headline that sums up the last ten years of the American (and other rich country's) workplace—and the next thirty years as well—it would be this: "That Job Is Gone!" That's the cold water I'd throw in the face of every man or woman who thinks his or her fu-ture can be understood by looking nostalgically to the past.

This is the new reality not only for blue-collar workers like Jared, but for all workers, young people just entering the workforce in rich countries as well as veteran professionals.

The forces that created this new high-stress environment are not mysterious.

The biggest factor is *globalization*. Westerners not only compete with other Americans and Europeans for the best jobs, they have to compete with a wave of smart, highly motivated candidates from India, China, and

---

* The exceptions here, of course, are the lifetime jobs that many teachers, police officers, firefighters, career soldiers, and other government employees may have.

eastern Europe. You only have to count the number of foreign students in America's most prestigious graduate programs to appreciate this.

Another factor is the dramatically *increased gap in compensation* between the top people in an organization and everyone else. CEOs and other C-level officers have been incredibly well rewarded by corporate America over the past twenty years. Their income has increased at a much greater pace than that of middle managers and staff professionals. That makes the competition for the top jobs more vital—and brutal too. With more people competing at the narrow top of the pyramid, everyone works harder and longer.

A third factor is *decreased job security.* In the early 1980s, I did a study of dismissals at IBM. At that time, IBM would always fire people for ethical violations, but almost no one was fired for poor performance. If you wore a white shirt, showed up, and met minimal expectations, you had a job for life. As IBM's profits dwindled, then-CEO John Akers faced increased pressure from stockholders to change IBM. His hesitation to move away from IBM's full-employment practice was one reason he was ousted. But IBM's lack of tough performance standards was commonplace at the time, no different than what was happening at AT&T, General Motors, Eastman Kodak, and other "blue chip" pillars of corporate America. All that has changed now, of course. Along with the carrot of increased rewards, managers and professionals live with the stick of losing their jobs. Nonperformance can bring severe and immediate punishment. We see this most dramatically in a marked decline in mid-level work, a "hollowing out" of the middle class. The shortage of mid-level jobs has only widened the gap between society's economic winners and losers.

Another factor is the steady erosion in the past twenty years of *company-funded guaranteed health-care and retirement security.* This affects professionals as well as wage earners, meaning that everyone worries more about long-term security. The result: People are not only working much harder, they're facing the prospect of working much longer.

A fifth factor is the *global financial crisis* that began in 2008. It won't last forever (history tells us this), but it won't let us go back to business as usual either (history tells us this too). And for the immediate future, it has heightened the already-present fear in the workplace—fear of losing a job, or a home, or of ever finding high-quality professional work again.

The sixth and perhaps most lethal factor, ironically, is *new technology*. It seems ridiculous now that people believed new technology would lead to more leisure time and fewer hours at work. Instead, new technology, hand in hand with globalization, has created a 24/7 world where work never seems to stop. Professionals everywhere are glued to their cell phones, laptops, and PDAs—always reachable, always in a state of high alert, always prepared to outwork their rivals. This attitude has blurred the boundaries between work and home, creating that sad oxymoron, the "working vacation."

The result is a new breed of professional employee, more driven and hardworking yet more insecure than ever before. For employees who love what they do—and find meaning in their work—long hours are not an issue. For employees who lack Mojo, the world of work can begin to resemble a "new-age professional hell." Young professionals will work longer hours, even if they don't like their jobs—it's not like the old days when they could have a "second life" outside of work and find meaning and happiness.

When you work sixty to eighty hours a week, and "work-life" balance is defined as what happens outside of "work," there won't be much left for a great "life."

In this new world, Mojo is both harder to attain and more important to keep. When your competition is already responding to a tough new environment by working harder and longer, you need unique tools to separate yourself from the throng. Mojo will not be an option for professionals. It will become more and more of a requirement. The specific strategies and actions that I cover in the next section, "Your Mojo Tool Kit," are designed to help you create and maintain your Mojo—in a challenging new world.

Your Mojo
Tool Kit

CHAPTER 11

Change You or Change It

I hope I didn't scare you too much at the end of the previous section by coloring the workplace with so many challenges that you now feel lucky just to hang on to your job.

It's not *that* bad.

If you step back, you'll discover that you're still in control of your life and destiny. You have the power to create significant positive change.

Which begs the next question: *What can you change?* The answer is simple: You can change either You or It.

By You, I mean how you think, how you feel, what you say—basically everything about you that's under your control.

It, on the other hand, refers to any influencing forces in your life that are not you. It could be another individual, or a group of people, or a job, or a place, or a relationship, or the results of a choice you made in the past that needs undoing. It is everything that's not You.

It's a stark unambiguous binary. Yet a lot of us make the wrong choice. We try to change It when we should be changing something about ourselves—and vice versa.

For example, we all know a few people who hate their companies. It's interesting to watch how people deal with this emotion.

Some people do nothing. They stoically endure the situation. But doing nothing is not much of an option if your aim is to elevate your Mojo. You're choosing the status quo. You're electing to stay miserable rather than try to be happy. You're electing to do meaningless work instead of meaningful work. That's not change of any kind.

Some people find another job. They remove themselves from the offending employer and seek out a new environment. It's risky (you never know how your next company will turn out), but it's changing It in its purest form. If things are bad enough, why not try it?

Some people alter their attitude toward the company. They assess why they feel the way they do and try to find a new way to interact with their coworkers. For example, you may resent the fact that your employer calls you about business some nights or weekends. You may initially believe that this is rude and invasive, not to mention socially disruptive. You may choose to change yourself and make peace by accepting that your company sees no other options. You may mentally readjust what you regard as your "working hours." That's changing You. If you have no choice, and see no options, make peace with what is.

Some people positively and proactively change their work environment. They treat decision makers with respect, yet "challenge up" on important issues. They make a positive difference in their work environment. They respect final decisions that cannot be changed, yet realize that they can impact many decisions that are "in progress" and *can* be changed.

Many people do none of the above. Instead they whine and complain about their employers, as if voicing their resentment will miraculously inspire the company to change. What are the odds of that happening? (Answer: Slim to none.) The cartoonist Scott Adams, creator of *Dilbert,* has built a thriving career depicting people who make this choice when confronted with changing You or It. His prisoners of cubicle culture never change; they just whine. It makes for a trenchant, biting, funny cartoon strip, filled with cynicism and dark insights into the workplace, but it's not an appealing high-Mojo place to be in real life.

Changing You is not inherently preferable or easier than changing It (and vice versa). The best approach depends on the situation.

Once you're aware of this "You or It" dichotomy, you begin to see manifestations everywhere and you begin to realize its impact on Mojo. You see that in all work and personal situations, Mojo is a function of the relationship between who you are (i.e., You) and your situation (i.e., It). If you cannot change You, Mojo is influenced by your relationship to It. If you cannot change It, Mojo is influenced by your relationship to You. It's your choice.

It is your life. If your Mojo is suffering, no one can make the "you vs. it" decision for you. My only suggestion is that you become clear on your own values and make a thoughtful decision.

One of my friends has a son named Will whose goal was a career in magazines. Immediately after graduating from college in 2008, in the heart of the most disruptive time in the history of magazine publishing, he got an entry-level job at a major weekly in New York City. He got decent pay and benefits, and worked directly for an editor in chief he genuinely liked and admired. His Mojo was high. Landing your first real job in a dream situation will do that to your Mojo score. Six months later the British owners fired Will's boss—and Will too. This was in early 2009, when magazines were going out of business on a daily basis and unemployment in New York City was in the double digits. Will had no success finding another job. He had to move back in with his parents, collect unemployment, and had no prospects for finding work—a perfect scenario for Nojo.

Here's where Will's story takes an interesting turn.

Some people would wallow in self-criticism at a time like this; they'd assume that it was something about them that was damaging their job search. So, in other words, they'd try to change You. They'd pretend to be someone they were not in order to get hired somewhere.

Other people would whine. They'd convince themselves that getting fired was not their fault, that it was a rotten time to look for a job, that the situation was out of their control. They'd hope something would turn up.

Will did neither. Instead, he changed It. Since finding a job was virtually impossible, he decided to create a new job for himself: He'd go to law school. His parents were aghast. They'd never imagined their son as a lawyer, and they weren't prepared to pay the six-figure bill for three years of law school. But Will had that worked out, at least in theory. He would use his considerable downtime to study hard for the LSAT. If he scored high enough, a school would give him a scholarship. (Worst case, he'd get a student loan.) In effect, his plan was to get paid for going to law school. In the meantime, he'd sit out one of the worst job environments in decades. And when he graduated three years later, he'd have a professional degree and maybe the job market would be healthier.

It's too soon to tell if all this will work out according to plan, but Will's in law school now, with a full scholarship. And he's happy about it. His Mojo is high. That can happen when you assess a low-Mojo situation and change something fundamental about . . . It.

Contrast this with Bob, a lawyer in his mid-forties whom I met at a conference. Bob is a solo practitioner in the same upstate New York town that he grew up in. He used to practice real estate law, but when the real estate market dried up in his area, he switched to family law—meaning he handles divorces and custody battles. It's one of the nastier corners of the law. You're dealing with angry spouses, tracking down deadbeat dads who don't pay their child support, and advocating in family court for kids who don't want to be with either parent, and don't particularly trust you either. It's a radical departure from the more predictable ups and downs of real estate closings. As Bob animatedly described his job, he spotted a friend and waved hello.

"That's my former law partner," he explained. "I envy him. He loves being a lawyer. I hate it."

"Why?" I asked.

"He gets a kick out of being an adversary, engaging in battle with other lawyers. He can tell them to go to hell and have a drink with them an hour later. It's sport to him. I can't do that. I can't separate myself from all the harsh words. And I'm not built for fighting."

"It sounds like you're in the wrong line of work," I said.

"I know," he said with a sigh, and then his voice trailed off into silence.

Bob was a walking, talking paragon of low Mojo, and he had no clue how to change his life. He was trapped in a job of his own choosing (no one forced him into family law) but he loathed it. Perhaps he could have adjusted his personality to become more of a legal scrapper, someone who savored the jousting in family court. That would have been changing the You in his life (although I suspect it also would have been as unlikely as me becoming someone who likes to manage people and review balance sheets). Alternatively, he could have changed It. He could have begun cultivating new clients as he prepared to segue into a more amenable area of the law; he'd done it once before. But he was doing neither, locked in place, sighing and whining to strangers like me.

These are two random anecdotes about people I know. But they could be people we all know. There are millions of people in America in the same shoes as Will and Bob.

Hundreds of thousands of recent graduates are sitting at desks or at home confused about what they want to do in life. Or they may feel like victims because they're entering a job market at its lowest ebb, or because they feel paralyzed in a job that is not the job they dreamed of. But most of them are lucky because they're young. They have time to make mistakes and recover from them. They're young enough that they can not only change It, but they can handle a complete You makeover. They can change how they think, communicate, feel; they can develop skills that they never considered, build a network of new friends, and create a new identity.

It's not as easy for people like Bob, past age forty, with at least two decades of work under their belt, with families, debts, responsibilities, and a bunch of behavioral habits that may be hard to break. They can't make radical changes—to You or It—without considering the costs and consequences to the people who depend on them. Those are formidable obstacles. It explains why a smart fellow like Bob, with a family and a mortgage, sighs about the dead end he's in rather than trying to break out of it.

As for Will, the law student, his choice is not particularly original (thousands of young people, many of whom don't really want to be lawyers, attend law school as a placeholder when they don't know what else to do). And it's risky. He may hate law school or there still might not be a job for him when he graduates in three years. But he's a step ahead of many people—because he's making a change.

The following is a list of specific actions that can help you attack the challenge of changing You or It. They fit in what I call your Mojo Tool Kit, because they are tools, not tricks of the mind or magical potions. Like tools, they don't work unless you grab them in your hands and use them. They are:

- **Establish Criteria That Matter to You**: Setting ground rules for your life can start you on the path toward great Mojo.

- **Find Out Where You're Living**: "Where" is defined by how we balance short-term satisfaction and long-term benefit at work and at home.

- **Be the Optimist in the Room**: There's power in "going for it" and not being afraid to look foolish.

- **Take Away One Thing**: How would life look if you eliminated something big from your daily schedule?

- **Rebuild One Brick at a Time**: A wall is built one brick at a time. So's your Mojo.

- **Live Your Mission in the Small Moments Too**: The *small* moments in our lives can make *big* statements about who we are.

- **Swim in the Blue Water**: A new way to win can be to *change the game!*

- **When to Stay, When to Go**: It's better to jump than be pushed.

- **Hello, Good-bye**: How to say "hello" and prepare for "good-bye."

- **Adopt a Metrics System**: How personally created stats reveal what you need to know.

- **Reduce This Number**: It's the percentage of time we spend on boasting or criticizing—by ourselves and others.

- **Influence Up as Well as Down**: Turn important decision makers into your best customers.

- **Name It, Frame It, Claim It**: Naming what we do can help us enhance how we do it.

- **Give Your Friends a Lifetime Pass**: Friends can be more forgiving than we deserve—give them a break.

I've organized these actions into four chapters, each corresponding to one of the four building blocks of Mojo: Identity, Achievement, Reputation, and Acceptance.

Thus, if your issue is Acceptance—dealing with problems that are beyond your control—you might find the recommended action in "Give Your Friends a Lifetime Pass" immediately helpful. You're changing something about You.

If your issue is Reputation—you want the world's opinion of you to match your own—a remedial strategy can be found in "When to Stay, When to Go." You're changing It.

You get the picture. Each action initiates a change in You or It.

I can't predict how many of these actions are apt for you. We all have different issues. But I suspect we can all learn something from each one, so don't skip around. I would suggest reading them in order. And pay strict attention to the first one, on developing personal criteria. All of us could do better at that.

CHAPTER 12

Identity: Making Sense of Who You Are

In this chapter we begin with four tools that can help reshape or refine the "you" that you present to the world. Tool #1 stresses the importance of criteria for how you choose to live your life. Tool #2 will help you define the short-term satisfaction and long-term benefit that you're pursuing. Tool #3 is about shedding pessimism (one of the classic challenges in any identity change). Tool #4 offers a playful (and serious) exercise about whom you would be if you removed one feature.

TOOL #1: Establish Criteria That Matter to You

When people lose Mojo, the cause can often be traced to a rootless sense of mission. They lack clear goals. They don't target opportunities. They can't decide on simple criteria for how they define their lives. And so they wander aimlessly, or spin in circles, or stand in place (which in a rapidly changing world actually amounts to falling behind).

That's why I've positioned this as the first course of action in your Mojo Tool Kit. I want readers to reclaim the power of establishing their own criteria for meaning and happiness in their lives. It's the best way to identify what matters.

A lot of us, especially if we work *for other people* rather than *for ourselves,* have forgotten that we have the choice to set our own goals. Instead, we operate under criteria handed to us by others that lure us into mindlessly running with the herd. When this happens, we rarely take the opportunity to set our own criteria.

The best thing about having criteria is that it forces you to be precise—in what you do and how you hold yourself accountable afterward. It's the difference between saying, "I'd be happier if I spent more time with my kids" and "I am going to spend at least four hours a week with each of my kids." The former statement is vague—and therefore meaningless. What's "more time" mean? One minute more than you're spending now? How will that tiny incremental improvement matter to your kids—or you? On the other hand, "four hours" is specific and measurable. It creates accountability. You either hit the target or miss. And if you hit the target, you reward yourself with an invisible gold medal every week. That makes you feel good about yourself on the inside—and this quickly shows on the outside, especially to the people who really matter, namely your kids. That's how Mojo happens. It's not magical; it only seems that way.

A few years ago I was working with a woman named Barbara, who appeared to be a highly motivated high-achieving executive at a marketing firm—except—in reality—she was miserable. When I asked her what was making her miserable, she couldn't really pin it down. She liked most of her work, she liked her colleagues, she was good at her job, and she saw a clear growth path in her career.

"Okay," I said, "let's turn it upside down. If you don't know what's making you unhappy, why don't you tell me what would make you happy?"

"That's easy," she said. "Happy would be—not having to go to any meetings that I do not want to attend."

That was a breakthrough for Barbara, because suddenly she had articulated a very specific criterion for her working life. It was all about meetings. She hated them. But it was more than that. What Barbara was chafing at was a lack of autonomy and self-direction.

So she quit her job and set herself up as a consultant, working out of her home. This wasn't just a shift into telecommuting (which is basically keeping your job but doing it at home). She was now self-employed, which can be risky and stressful. But she was also completely in control of her time. Instead of endless meetings, she communicated with clients by e-mail and phone, and when she needed a face-to-face with anyone, it was *her* choice. Acting on her simple criterion not only removed the forced attendance at pointless meetings, but it also cut out the daily commute into the office and her obligatory presence on equally fruitless conference calls—all of which helped to liberate three or four previously occupied hours from her day.

When I tracked her down eighteen months later, she was no longer working at home. Her business had grown so quickly that she'd opened an office a few minutes away from home and now employed four people. "But still no unnecessary meetings," she said. "My staff is not complaining."*

Barbara's story is neither unique nor extraordinary. There are, after all, millions of refugees from the corporate world who are working out of their homes or in small offices. What makes her special is the spark that initiated her new life change—namely, identifying a criterion that made a difference. When you articulate a criterion for leading your life, it dictates many of the major choices that follow, closing some doors but opening others.

It doesn't matter what area you apply criteria to, as long as it helps *you* to identify what will make you find happiness and meaning.

Some people have strict criteria about time management. What makes them happy is the smooth, uninterrupted flow of their carefully calibrated day. So they have rules to maintain that happy pace. They don't let unscheduled phone calls run longer than five minutes. They won't live more than a thirty-minute commute from their job. They only fly nonstop. They won't let lunches run longer than ninety minutes (if a meal's going to take hours, let it be dinner). They won't read a book that's more than four hundred pages, or a memo that can't be digested down to one page. And so on. We've all met people like this. Perhaps they're a little obsessive-compulsive about the clock, but they're a step ahead of us because at least they have criteria.

Some people have criteria about the kind of work they're willing to do. For example, they'll only work on projects that pay X dollars or more. Or because they hate cold weather, they'll only work in a warm climate. Or they'll only take on work that conforms to their idea of a sane family life. A successful opera singer, whose career is essentially a never-ending sched-

---

* I'm the polar opposite of Barbara when it comes to meetings. I'll make time to see anyone who asks to meet with me. My job is understanding interpersonal behavior, so talking to new people is a good way of getting fresh material. If someone is going to make me smarter, I've got all the time in the world for them. My criterion is, *Worst case, it won't make me dumber.*

ule of rehearsing and performing for three or four weeks at a time with a different opera company in a different city around the world, once told me that, when his two kids were growing up, his principal career criterion was to turn down engagements that took him away from home for more than two consecutive weeks (unless he could bring his family with him). That was the longest time he could stand to be apart from them without feeling guilty—and without worrying that they'd "forget" him. It limited his fees and his international bookings, but it was a criterion that worked for him. He could sacrifice some prestigious appearances, but not his responsibility as a father. A brave choice, made easier for everyone around him because of his specific criterion.

Some of our most useful criteria exist to help us deal with the annoyances or hazards of our jobs. Doctors are a good example of this. I know more than a few doctors who significantly improved their Mojo by adopting one criterion for their medical practice: *They refused to deal with the complex maze of insurance coverage that governed their practice or restricted their income.* A criterion like that dictates serious change in the medicine you practice, and it has made doctors creative and entrepreneurial (high Mojo) rather than pawns in a no-win game (low Mojo). Some became plastic surgeons, where all their patients pay in cash. Some shifted into academic medicine, avoiding the nuisances of clinical practice. One internist I know became a specialist in performing colonoscopies—and only colonoscopies. Instead of seeing a parade of patients of all ages and ailments, all with different insurance coverage, he only has to deal with insurance for one procedure.

I love my own doctor! He clearly determined his criteria for success and decided to set up a private practice. I pay him a little extra money—yet still a very reasonable amount—to get a physical exam every year and never wait in line. His limited practice enables him to take the time to talk with me about my health. He calls me up immediately when test scores come back—and does whatever he can to help me stay healthy. He is like a "new and improved" version of the old family doctor, which is exactly what he set out to be. His criteria are not for every doctor, but they work for him. (In the same way, my criteria are not for every patient, but they work for me.)

Peter Drucker was one of the world's experts at helping organizations define their mission. I once asked Peter (who was then in his nineties),

"What is your mission?" He replied without hesitation, "My mission is to help other people achieve their goals—assuming they are not immoral or unethical." He then laughed and jokingly added, "At my age I don't care if they are illegal!"

Peter was joking, but he was making a point about having a code for the people we let into our lives. Here was a man who could have worked with the narrowest, most elite cohort of CEOs, government leaders, and billionaires—and instead his criteria were *expanding* his population of potential clients. In his latest years, a lot of his best work was done with non-profit organizations who were engaged in human services.

What's strange is that most of us in business apply criteria to people all the time. We do it when we hire someone to work for us. We'll insist on a résumé and references. We'll make them take tests. We'll interview them face-to-face, often asking intrusive questions that would be rude in a normal social setting. We do all this because we're looking for a candidate that most closely matches the criteria we have in our mind.

A bigger question is why don't we apply the same rigor to the people up and down the food chain who can profoundly influence our careers and happiness? Why don't we have "hiring criteria" for the kind of boss we're willing to work for, or the clients we'll take on, or the colleagues we partner up with on a project? The biggest question is why don't we apply the same vigor to ourselves?

In my previous book, *What Got You Here Won't Get You There*, I outlined the Four Commitments I requested from the coworkers who provided feedback about my clients. These coworkers were the people who not only told me what the executive was doing wrong, they would be the ones twelve to eighteen months down the road who would be determining if my coaching was a success—and if I got paid. Thus, I work hard at "qualifying" the people rating my work. Otherwise, the entire coaching process may be poisoned, and I'm wasting my time. I ask them to commit to:

1. Let go of the past (helping my clients focus on a future they can change—not a past they cannot change)
2. Tell the truth (letting my clients know the truth and not just telling them "what they want to hear")

3. Be supportive and helpful (giving my clients encouragement, not cynicism or sarcasm)

4. Pick something to improve yourself (so everyone has some skin in the game and is focused on improving rather than judging)

In a very few cases, key stakeholders of my clients admit that they do not want to meet these criteria. They admit that they are angry and do not want to help my clients try to improve. In these cases, I ask them to merely refrain from the confidential evaluation that occurs at the end of my coaching process. I note that since they are unwilling to give my clients a fair chance—no matter what my clients do to change—they should not participate in judging my clients' improvement. Although this has only occurred in a few rare cases, in each case the stakeholder said that I was being fair in my criteria—and since they did not want to help my client, they agreed that they should not be judging my client.

It took me a few years of trial and error to come up with the Four Commitments, but they provide a workable model for the kind of criteria I'm talking about. If you're unhappy in your job, list a few qualities of a job that *would* make you happy. If you're unhappy with your boss, list some qualities of your ideal boss. If you don't like where you're living, establish the criteria of your ideal place to live. If you don't like the people around you, picture the attributes of people you would like to have as friends. This is not a tough assignment. It's life planning at its most basic. Yet I wonder how many people have actually written down a checklist of their ideal boss or their criteria for a friend.

People with lots of Mojo did not stumble upon their Mojo by accident. They had a good idea of what and where and who would increase their chances of finding meaning and happiness. They may not have called it "criteria" or formally written it down (although I bet a lot of them have done so), but at some point they locked down specifically what matters to them.

Before you can establish or regain your Mojo, you first have to imagine what it looks like and what it takes to get there. If you write it down, that's your criteria. It's as good a place to start as anything I can imagine.

TOOL #2:
Find Out Where You're "Living"

No, I don't mean get a map and pinpoint your street address. We all know where we sleep at night.

But a lot of us aren't fully aware of where we "live" emotionally all day long, especially in relation to the meaning and happiness we derive from our work. If we're remotely ambitious and self-aware, we're constantly questioning our "location." Are we on the right path? Are we in the right place? Is it time to move on? What's the best route to the next place? And will I be happier when I get there?

We don't broadcast these questions publicly—we might share such thoughts with a spouse or best friend—but they loiter in our minds and they make us doubt if our personal GPS is working properly.

In analyzing our relationship to our work—how we're spending it professionally and personally—all of us, consciously or not, run everything through two filters: short-term satisfaction (or happiness) and long-term benefit (or meaning). Both have value. After all, it can be disappointing to live our lives with no pleasure in the here and now, but it can also be unfulfilling to live only for today with no regard for the future. Neither misery nor emptiness is a desirable option for most human beings!

When we ask ourselves questions like "Does this activity make me happy?" we're really attempting to measure the short-term satisfaction we get from an activity. When we ask ourselves, "Are the results achieved from this activity worth my effort and will they pay off some day?" we're really trying to measure that activity's long-term positive impact or meaning to us. Some of it is guessing, some of it is hoping, but there's not much in our lives that isn't overshadowed by a sense that the clock is ticking, the calendar pages are flipping, and time is passing. And we want to know whether we're living in the short-term or the long-term.

Basically, all of us, at any point in time, are "living" in one of the five following modes, which reflect the balance between our need for short-term satisfaction and our desire for long-term benefit. Which one applies to you for most of your life?

My daughter, Dr. Kelly Goldsmith, has a Ph.D. in Marketing from Yale and is now an assistant professor of Marketing at Northwestern Uni-

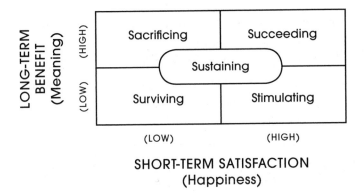

SHORT-TERM SATISFACTION
(Happiness)

versity's Kellogg School of Management. Kelly and I developed the Mojo Survey to help us understand how respondents experience meaning and happiness (at work and home). (To complete this survey, just go to www .MojoTheBook.com) Our Mojo survey participants were asked to describe elements of work and home life that scored high or low in meaning and happiness. Thousands of respondents have already completed the survey. We also asked participants to let us know how much time they were spending in various categories. We then compared our results with their overall satisfaction with life at work and outside of work. I will discuss our findings as we continue. (See Appendix II for a more detailed discussion of our Mojo Survey findings.)

Surviving is our term for activities that score low on short-term satisfaction and low on long-term benefit. Typically, these are activities that we feel we have to do in order just to get by. When our Mojo survey respondents were asked to describe "surviving" activities, at work and home, the term "chores" was frequently used. We all have "chores" that we have to do—both at work and at home. Charles Dickens wrote often about poor people whose lives were dominated by hard work, little joy, and not much to show for all of their efforts. A life such as this, spent primarily in surviving mode, would be a hard life indeed.

Stimulating describes activities that score high in short-term satisfaction but low in long-term benefit. Watching TV, movies, or athletic contests were frequently mentioned by participants in our survey as "stimulating" activities. They may provide short-term satisfaction but they have little potential for long-term benefit. Non-business chatting with coworkers is another: fun in the short term but not career-enhancing in the long term. A life spent primarily on stimulating activities could provide a lot of short-term pleasure but still be headed nowhere.

Sacrificing describes activities that score low in short-term satisfaction but high in long-term benefit. An extreme example is dedicating your life to work that you hate because you feel like you "have to" in order to achieve a larger goal (e.g., feeding your family, sending your kids to college, saving for retirement). A more common example is setting aside an hour a day to exercise (when you don't feel like it) to improve your long-term health. At work, sacrificing might be spending extra hours on a project you don't like to enhance your career prospects. A life spent primarily in sacrificing mode would be the life of a martyr—lots of achievement but little joy.

Sustaining is for activities that produce moderate amounts of short-term satisfaction and lead to moderate long-term benefits. Responding to professional emails might be a classic sustaining activity in the Internet age. Sustaining activities are moderately interesting (not thrilling), and usually produce moderate long-term but hardly life-changing benefits. At home, the day-to-day activities of living may often fall into the "sustaining" category. At work, completing mid-level assignments or required reading were listed as "sustaining" by survey participants. A life spent primarily on sustaining activities would be okay—not great, but not much to complain about.

Succeeding describes activities that score high on both short-term satisfaction and long-term benefits. These are activities that we love to do and get great benefit from doing. We simultaneously find happiness and meaning. At work, people who spend a lot of time in the succeeding box feel that they have the ideal job suited to their talents and that they achieve long-term benefits that matter to them. At home, a parent may be spending hours with a child, which the parent enjoys immensely (it doesn't feel like sacrificing), while attaching great value to the long-term benefit it brings to the child (it's not just stimulating). A life spent primarily in succeeding mode is a life filled with both accomplishment and joy.

Only we can say whether we are truly deriving personal satisfaction and benefit from an activity. And the differences in perception among individuals can be head-spinning. An immigrant, for example, who leaves a poor country and comes to the United States where she works eighteen hours a day at two minimum-wage jobs may cherish those two jobs and have her eyes on the prize of saving every penny for her children's education. She may define her life as being spent largely in succeeding mode—filled with short-term happiness and long-term benefits—where someone else with more fortunate origins might regard such a life as bleak, the definition of surviving rather than succeeding.

At the other end of the professional scale, a CEO could resent her job and feel trapped because a sharp downturn has reduced her bonus and the value of her company's stock, which means she will have to work another couple of years to have the nest egg she told herself she needed to retire. Feeling forced to stay in the job, she might see herself in the surviving category. Another CEO in a similar situation might feel engaged and fulfilled at being given the chance to lead an organization through challenging times; it's the perfect definition of succeeding for her.

The point is, two people engaged in the same activity can have completely different perceptions of what the activity means to them. It's important to remember this as many of us face one of the most disruptive, turbulent work environments in decades. Suddenly, one person's surviving is another's succeeding—and vice versa.

I got a vivid lesson about this from Frank, the president of a two-branch savings and loan in Jasper, Georgia. Frank was driving through Prattville, Alabama, when he stopped for dinner at a LongHorn Steakhouse. It was packed, so Frank grabbed the last remaining seat at the bar.

Sitting there with twenty other people, waiting for the lone woman bartender to take his order of one Flo's Filet, medium rare, Frank had a moment to observe and listen. He focused on the bartender, wondering how long it would take her to notice him and get him something to drink. She was in her late thirties, he guessed, dressed in the same cowboy-shirt-and-jeans outfit as every other employee in the restaurant. But she was unlike any service provider he had ever seen. She didn't waste one step, one comment, one move along the bar. She took his order for a draft beer less than thirty seconds after he settled in his seat, asking, "Are you having dinner too?" Less than a minute later, she had plunked the beer, a bowl of peanuts, a menu, and the silverware in front of him—all while she was serving drinks and dinners to the twenty other patrons at the bar. She also handled the drink orders for the entire restaurant. And was responsible for making sure every takeout order was correct before it went out the door. She was a non-stop bundle of energy combined with an efficiency expert. And she was smart. When she fell behind, she knew precisely when and what to say to let each patron know that she hadn't forgotten him or her. She had the politician's gift of making everyone feel like the most important person in her world.

Frank was impressed. As he sliced up his filet, his first thought was that if there were a reality show for the best bartender in America, this woman could win.

Her name, he learned, was Cothy—like Cathy, only with an "o," she said.

He told her, "You're the most impressive bartender I've ever seen. You should come work for me at my bank in Georgia." It wasn't the drink talking. Frank was half-serious; someone this amazing could do anything.

She couldn't do that, she explained. "I'm divorced. I have an eight-year-old daughter and my mother at home. I couldn't just get up and leave them. Besides, you couldn't afford me."

"We pay pretty well in Georgia," Frank said.

Then she leaned over the bar and whispered, "Well, you're going to leave me a tip, right? Multiply your tip by sixty, then multiply that by five days a week, fifty weeks a year, and you're getting close to what I'd cost you." Frank did the math in his head and realized she was quite possibly out-earning him.

On paper, her résumé didn't sound promising: divorced, single mom, raising a daughter alone, living under the same roof with her mother, and working nights at a bar. For many people, that would fall somewhere between Sacrificing and Surviving. But this woman clearly loved what she was doing, and as a result did it so well that she could handle all her responsibilities, and then some. She had enough Mojo to convince a stranger to hire her on the spot. She was, without question, Succeeding.

As Frank got up from his meal, he tripled his usual tip. A small gesture, more a salute to a great worker than excessive generosity. Frank wanted to impress her, as she had impressed him, even though he knew he'd never pass through Prattville, Alabama, again. That's another thing about Mojo: it's infectious. When people pass their positive spirit to us, we feel like passing it back.

A great way to test your Mojo is to consider your life at work—then consider your life outside of work. What percent of your time is spent in each of the five categories? How can you increase your time in "succeeding"? Our research from the Mojo survey has provided a clear message. People who find happiness and meaning at work tend to be the same people that find happiness and meaning at home! In other words, our Mojo is coming from inside ourselves—as much as it is from what we are doing.

Our findings have also shown that, for the majority of people, the only way to increase overall satisfaction with life (both at work and outside work) is to increase *both* happiness and meaning. (See Appendixes I and II to review the Mojo Survey and read about some of our initial findings.)

TOOL #3:
Be the Optimist in the Room

When people initiate a personal campaign to improve themselves—for example, lose weight, shed a bad habit, exercise more, be nicer to their coworkers (or family members), run a marathon, learn a new language, play a musical instrument, elevate their Mojo—there is a high probability that they will fail.* At some point, early in the game or near the finish line, most people will abandon their campaign to get better.

Why do people give up? My daughter Kelly helped me review the research on goal achievement—and we came up with six major reasons:

1. **It takes longer than we thought.** Our need for instant gratification trumps our patience and discipline.

2. **It's more difficult than we thought.** Improvement is hard. If it were easy, we'd already be better.

---

* To cite one statistic: In 2006, *Men's Health* reported, 71 percent of Americans failed to achieve their fitness goals for the year. That's a whole lot of failure for something that's good for you, possibly pleasurable to do, and not necessarily difficult to achieve. Keep in mind, we're not talking about bench-pressing five hundred pounds or finishing the Ironman Triathlon in Hawaii. For most people a fitness goal is as modest a task as taking a thirty-minute walk every other morning. And yet more than two-thirds of us fail at it. In the vast landscape of self-betterment, failure, not success, is the default result.

3. **We have other things to do.** Distractions tempt us to take our eyes off the ball.

4. **We don't get the expected reward.** We lose weight but still can't get a date. We put in the extra effort, but the boss doesn't notice or care. This creates frustration rather than inspiration to persist.

5. **We declare victory too soon.** We lose a few pounds and say, "Let's order pizza."

6. **We have to do it forever.** It's not enough that we quit smoking. We can't have another cigarette for the rest of time. Maintenance is tough!

Most of us don't articulate these reasons to ourselves. We simply accept defeat and vow to do better the next time.

What's going on here is not a merely a failure of discipline, or an unrealistic vision of our future, or being overwhelmed by distractions or frustration. It's a crisis of optimism. After the first easy wave of success, when improvement gets harder to maintain, our efforts can seem more hopeless than hopeful. If you've ever gone on a diet and shed the first few pounds swiftly, only to hit a wall where the pounds don't fall off so quickly as you get nearer your target weight, you know the feeling. You lose your initial burst of optimism, and optimism is the fuel that drives the engine of change.

If you can maintain your optimism in the face of these six negative forces, you have an enormous advantage over most people. Optimism is not just a mind-set; it's a form of behavior that guides everything we do. It can be self-fulfilling. And it's contagious. The optimist in the room always has more influence than anyone else. People pick up on optimism and gravitate toward it. It's certainly more attractive (in the sense of *attracting* people toward your position) than pessimism.

I am not suggesting that you abandon realism. My suggestion is the opposite. Take a hard look at the six factors that will help derail your goal achievement. Know that they are coming. Then, when they happen (and they invariably will), you will realize that these challenges are normal and be more likely to "hang in there" and maintain your optimism.

An Executive Optimist

I saw the impact of optimism firsthand with my client Harlan. I wrote about Harlan in *What Got You Here Won't Get You There*. Harlan was a division chief at an industrial company who was leading thousands of people. He was given a challenge by his CEO—increase the positive impact that you are having *across* the company, not just in your division. He made more progress toward his goals than anyone I have ever coached, even though I spent very little time with him—and he was great to start with! I haven't discussed what happened to Harlan over the last four years.

One of the reasons Harlan achieved positive change so quickly was that he is an "up," cheerful, optimistic person. He sees change as an opportunity, not a challenge. A few people, on first meeting Harlan, may see such a relentlessly positive attitude and think it's an act. No one can be this upbeat, they think. It's not a Pollyanna sunniness, where Harlan is happy that the sky is blue and wouldn't it be great if we all just got along. You don't lead thousands of people without a realist's tough side. Harlan simply goes through life seeing the glass seven-eighths full rather than half-empty.

For a variety of reasons, beyond his control, Harlan was not promoted when the CEO slot opened up. For some this would be a Mojo destroyer, the end of a dream. For others, whining about "unfairness" or "lack of logic" could ensue.

But that wasn't Harlan. I talked with him several times during this rough period, and though he was disappointed, he acknowledged that given the circumstances, he accepted the decision. But his unflagging optimism guided his thinking and behavior. He had already labeled his unfortunate situation as "Stuff Happens"—and moved on. If he was feeling wounded, the scars were not showing. And he stayed in the job, doing a great job. He knew that headhunters were always looking for managers like him—who could run something big and knew how to motivate people. Those skills hadn't vanished. His identity and achievements were still intact. As for his reputation, the fact that he would never be CEO at this company was disappointing to him, but not a game breaker for the rest of the world. Although he loved his company, he felt free to consider options elsewhere. If he did leave, he knew that his direct reports wouldn't feel betrayed; they'd understand.

I wasn't sure if this was Harlan's relentless cheeriness talking, but he had years of great results that validated his optimism. Even if others don't know about our histories, optimism can be a difference maker. Believing in what we can achieve can improve your behavior and demeanor—and other people notice.

A year later, after saying no to several offers, Harlan accepted the CEO job at an even larger company. Although this company faced huge challenges, he has been tackling the assignment with his characteristically positive Mojo! Harlan never lost his positive spirit. He did not let one setback color his attitude toward work and life. This is one reason why so many of the employees at his new firm are thrilled that he is doing all he can to serve them, their customers, and their shareholders.

Harlan is not that unusual in his optimism—only in how wide he casts his net of hope. He isn't only optimistic about *his* future, he feels the same way (within reason) about *other* people's potential as well. That's why he can lead and others will follow. Optimism like his isn't merely infectious, it's positively radioactive.

The Optimism Bias

What's interesting about this is that many of us are already irrepressible optimists, at least when the subject is ourselves. Psychologists call this "optimism bias," and it's one of the more well-researched concepts in behavioral economics. When people judge their chances of experiencing a good outcome—landing a big account, getting promoted, having a successful marriage, making a good financial investment—they estimate their odds to be better than average. When they consider the chances of something bad happening—losing a big account, getting fired, getting divorced—they assume odds lower than what they estimate for others.

Optimism bias inflates our self-confidence. It is the reason 90 percent of drivers think they're above average behind the wheel of a car. It's why some years ago when my two partners and I estimated our individual contributions to our partnership, the total came to more than 150 percent.

It's why almost all newlyweds believe there is zero chance their marriage will end in divorce, even when they know that 50 percent of marriages self-destruct (this is true even for the newly *re*married, who have already been divorced at least once).

It's the reason most smokers, despite the surgeon general's warning of on every pack of cigarettes, believe they are less likely to die of lung cancer than most nonsmokers. Their optimism extends to believing that they are better than other people at cheating death!

It's the reason new restaurants in big cities continue to open, despite well-documented failure rates as high as 90 percent. Restaurateurs know the numbers, but they do not think they apply to them. In regarding ourselves, successful people tend to be optimists. (A good thing too. Without it, people wouldn't get married, or plunge their life savings into a start-up business, or devote ten years of research to developing a cancer drug. A society that doesn't take risks based on optimism is doomed.)

But something happens to our optimism when we stop evaluating ourselves and begin evaluating our peers' chances of succeeding. We're not as optimistic when we take ourselves out of the equation. In fact, we can become pessimists and cynics. As evidence, gauge your level of optimism when you present one of your cherished ideas in a meeting. It should be high (or how else would you have the courage to air the idea in public?). Compare that to your level of optimism when an arch-rival presents his or her best idea in the same meeting. It's probably not as high. You may greet the idea with skepticism, perhaps cynicism. You'll compare its value to your idea and find it wanting. Part of this is predictable envy and competitiveness; we don't mind a rival succeeding, but not more than us or at our expense. Part of it is the difficulty in being optimistic about someone else's abilities where we have no control over the outcome. But much of it is simply our failure to be generous in extending our optimism to others. That's the downside of optimism bias. We may see everything that could go wrong with the other person's idea while remaining blind to what could go wrong with ours. It's not a quality that we should hang on to.

If we can take the positive spirit inside us toward what *we* are doing now and extend it to what *other people* are doing—in other words, make our optimism contagious—then each of us has a better chance of becoming a person who can rise from a setback that might crumble others, a manager who doesn't yield to the standard cynicism and negativity, and a leader whom others will follow.

TOOL #4:
Take Away One Thing

Some years ago a friend lost the use of his vocal cords to throat cancer. It sent a chill through me—and made me wonder what I would do if I could no longer speak. Since two-thirds of my professional life involves either talking or listening (the other one-third is writing), I jotted down as many alternative careers as I could imagine. They ran the gamut from researcher to aid worker. I'm using "gamut" ironically, because my list was neither expansive nor imaginative. I was picking careers that were within my wheelhouse of experience. I wasn't stretching or staking out the impossible. I was engaging in a hypothetical exercise, not something real.

To my voiceless friend, however, the decision was real and immediate. He was a salesman, and a salesman who can't speak is operating at a huge disadvantage. He needed another career, one that didn't require speaking—and he preferred to be engaged in something he loved. Since both he and his wife were avid golfers, they started an online business buying and selling used golf equipment. "On the Internet, no one hears your voice," he e-mailed me.

The couple's timing was exquisite. They caught the late 1990s upsurge in both golf technology (which increased the trade-in activity in golf clubs) and Internet technology (anyone with a laptop and storage space could get into e-commerce). Within two months they were making a profit.

None of this would have happened without the components of cancer and golf—two words you don't usually see next to each other as part of a happy story. But the key here is the element of *subtraction*. It creates both *need* and *direction*. Losing the use of his voice created a need in my friend for a new path—and directed him to golf.

Most of us don't employ the power of subtraction in our lives—at least not until it's too late. That's why most people don't switch careers to something they're really passionate about until their career is taken away from them—and they have no choice but to dream with more daring.* *We don't change unless we're compelled to change.* Until then, most of us are prisoners of inertia, trapped in the status quo, rarely questioning our choices, never doing anything about it.

I'm not just talking about subtracting daily rituals or habits that have stealthily overtaken our lives—like going on a "media diet" (no TV, no radio, no Internet) or a "money diet" (no Starbucks, no personal trainer, no $800 shoes) for a month or so. However valuable, these are merely experiments in doing without. They're temporary sacrifices, not permanent changes. I'm talking about subtracting something that is a "big deal."

Barbara, the marketing executive mentioned earlier, hated meetings, so she subtracted them and rebuilt her work life accordingly. As a dean, I learned that I didn't enjoy managing people, so I left that job and developed a life with few full-time employees. My friend couldn't speak, so he subtracted the need for a voice from his next career.

In a world where addition is the customary method of rewarding ourselves—more money, more things, more friends, more productivity, more fun—subtraction is not the most obvious success strategy, or the first tool we reach for in our Mojo Tool Kit. But it can reshape our world in ways we cannot imagine.

I have always been impressed by the improbable career of the football broadcaster John Madden. Madden was a successful NFL football coach (he won the Super Bowl in 1977 with the Oakland Raiders) who gave up the coach's whistle for the broadcaster's microphone at age forty-two. This

---

* One of my favorite W. Somerset Maugham short stories is "The Verger." It involves a middle-aged man named Albert who has spent most of his adult life as a "verger," or vicar's assistant, at a posh church, St. Peter's, Neville Square, in London. When church leaders discover that Albert cannot read or write, he's fired. As he's walking home that night, confused about what to do next, Albert hankers for a cigarette. But he can't find a shop to buy a pack. He finds that odd, musing that he can't be the only man in London who walks along this street and wants a cigarette.

So he leases a storefront on the street and sets himself up as a tobacconist and newsagent. It's a success, so he opens a shop on another street. Then another. Within ten years he owns ten shops. He's a wealthy man, collecting the week's receipts himself and depositing them in the bank.

One day the bank manager asks Albert to sign some transfer papers. Albert shocks the banker by admitting that he can't read or write.

"Do you mean to say that you've amassed a fortune without being able to read or write?" asks the banker. "Good God, man, what would you be now if you had been able to?"

"I'd be verger of St. Peter's, Neville Square," he says.

was not a slam-dunk career switch back in 1979. Ex-coaches in the broadcast booth were not the commonplace thing they are today. Plus, Madden's extra-large bull-in-a-china-shop personality was a radical departure from the usual smooth and soothing announcer voices that issued then from our TV sets.

Madden had only one self-imposed restriction for doing his new job: Because of claustrophobia, he wouldn't fly on a plane. He'd have to get around from game to game each Sunday during the NFL season using America's roads and highways. He literally subtracted the fastest, most efficient mode of travel from a job that required extensive travel.

Like the proverbial butterfly who flaps its wings in China in March, thus changing hurricane patterns over the Atlantic in August, Madden's "no fly" rule dictated and shaped much of what followed in his career.

For one thing, it forced Madden to get a bus—at first a modest vehicle, eventually a luxuriously appointed corporate-sponsored home on wheels known as the Maddencruiser—to take him every week from his home in Northern California to Dallas and New York and Washington and other NFL towns. On a cross-country trip, he'd be on the bus for nearly three days of straight travel. As an ex-coach, Madden loved to watch game films, studying teams' strategies and players' tendencies. On the bus, he had all the time in the world, with no distractions, to indulge his passion for game footage. This gave him a big edge over other broadcasters who could not or would not watch as much film as Madden. And it showed on television. Madden's insights and analysis of each play— while most of us were watching the ball, Madden could literally see what all twenty-two players on the field were doing each play—quickly set him apart as the smartest voice in the game. Eventually, he became the highest paid sportscaster in the world (with lots of time off from February through July).

Madden's reputation as a blunt, insightful analyst made him the perfect choice in 1988 to get involved in the burgeoning field of video games. He put his name and voice on a game called *Madden NFL,* which is updated annually and remains the top-selling sports video game in America (with more than six million units sold annually). The video game, with its built-in numerical rankings for each NFL player, has "educated" at least two generations of football fans about the NFL and is a big factor in the growth of fantasy football.

Subtracting flying from his life had one other effect on Madden. While the rest of us were taking jets across America, he was seeing the nation at ground level. He wasn't bypassing the so-called "fly-over" states; he was driving through them—and stopping the Maddencruiser whenever he arrived in a new town. It gave him a unique perspective on the nation's citizens and the people who love football. This isn't the only reason he evolved into such a successful pitchman in TV commercials, but this "common touch" that he developed on the road couldn't have hurt.

By the time Madden retired at age seventy-three in April 2009, saying simply, "It's time," he had achieved one of the most popular and lucrative broadcast careers in television history. I cannot believe he would have ended up in the same place if he had taken a plane.

The untapped power of subtraction is within your grasp. It's as easy as saying to yourself, *My life might actually be better if I took away_____.* And filling in the blank.

The answer, of course, is up to you. Some people might choose to subtract an annoying person. Some people might subtract a professional activity, like a lengthy commute or a scheduled weekly meeting. Some people might eliminate a recreational activity that is less fun than it used to be.

The only thing holding you back is your imagination and daring. There are so many things we can lose in our daily lives without harming our Mojo that it's inexcusable if we can't identify *one item* to toss away to increase our Mojo.

Even try the experiment by tossing away something that you do like! You don't actually have to give it up, but the exercise of asking yourself "What would I do if I knew I had to give this up?" will inspire your creativity—and, who knows, it might even increase your Mojo!

CHAPTER 13

Achievement: Making It Easier to Get Things Done

This chapter offers courses of action that put our achievements in sharper relief. Tool #5 attacks your greatest challenge: getting started. Tool #6 references the value of doing the little things that aren't so little. And Tool #7 encourages you to get beyond incremental improvement—and start innovating.

TOOL #5: Rebuild One Brick at a Time

Anne Lamott took the title for *Bird by Bird,* her wonderful book on writing, from one of her father's teachable moments. Here's how Lamott tells it:

> My older brother, who was ten years old at the time, was trying to get a report written that he'd had three months to write. It was due the next day. We were out at our family cabin in Bolinas, and he was at the kitchen table close to tears, surrounded by binder paper and pencils and unopened books on birds, immobilized by the hugeness of the task ahead. Then my father sat down beside him, put his arm around my brother's shoulder, and said, "Bird by bird, buddy. Just take it bird by bird."

When we feel that we've lost our Mojo, the thought of restoring it can seem a daunting task, as fearsome and paralyzing as the task faced by a child who must write a report that he has put off until the last minute. We don't know where to begin, we wish we had more time, we cannot see the finish line, and we have no confidence that we can reach it.

At that moment, the notion of rebuilding our Mojo "bird by bird" not only makes sense but provides us with enough psychic comfort that we can actually accomplish the toughest part of any "creative" endeavor: We can begin.

It's a common anxiety that I have experienced even with super-successful clients (who are rarely intimidated by a challenge) when they have to change their behavior. When I tell them it's a twelve- to eighteen-month process, they always think they can change more quickly—in a matter of weeks.

I tell them, "It's not about you. It's about the people around you. *They* need twelve to eighteen months to accept that you have changed." That's when the anxiety kicks in. They're sure they can change, but not so sure that others will see it.

The image I use with my clients to deal with long-term processes like changing behavior (or recapturing Mojo) is a brick—as in building a wall. You lay down one brick, then another, and before you know it, you have a wall.

Birds or bricks (what is it about goal-setting that calls up metaphors?)—it doesn't matter what imagery you employ to get started and keep going, the concept is the same: You're aiming for *serial achievements*. In order to show people who you are *now*, you can't rely on one-off gestures. They end up looking like stunts. (Imagine a rude coworker who's suddenly nice to you. The first time this happens you wonder, *Huh? What got into him?* The second time becomes a signal to pay attention. The third time a pattern begins to form in your mind. It's only until the nice behavior is repeated a dozen or more times in a row, without any flare-ups of rudeness, that you begin to accept that the change is real.) You have to string successes together. If you provide people with *continuity*, however trivial or feeble, they will notice. When they see a pattern of repeat positive behavior, they begin to understand what you're doing—and they accept a new you. This is how reputations are rebuilt. (Remember, brick walls are made up of lots of bricks.)

They don't have to be big splashy successes (and keep in mind, success is defined by you). They just have to be achieved in an observable sequence.

A great example of this comes from the actor Michael Caine* recounting how he overcame the disadvantages of his accent and social class—brick by brick—when he broke into the film business:

> To be a movie star you have to invent yourself. I was a Cockney boy and obviously didn't fit anybody's idea of what an actor was supposed to be, so I decided to put together elements that added up to a memorable package. I got myself seen around the "in" spots, wearing glasses and smoking a cigar. I became known as "that guy who wears glasses and smokes a cigar." Then people began to say, "He plays working class parts." Suddenly I was "that working class actor who wears glasses and smokes a cigar." Then word spread that I was quite amenable, so I became "that easy-to-work-with working-class actor who wears glasses and smokes a cigar." It was the truth, but I had quite consciously assembled the truth so nobody could miss it. I did for myself what the major studios used to do for the contract actors. I created an image.

These are some rules to consider so you finish what you've started and people take note.

First rule: Stop trying to be an oracle. Stop waiting for more information or for better circumstances before you get started. Anyone who thinks he or she can predict what will happen five years down the road is delusional. Change happens too quickly now. So stop straining to see into a future that is beyond your vision. We never have *all* the information we need; circumstances are rarely *perfect*. E. L. Doctorow, author of *Ragtime*, once said that "Writing a novel is like driving a car at night. You can only see as far as your headlights, but you can make the whole trip that way." It's the same with reestablishing your Mojo. You may not think you have all the tools and information you need to effect a change, but you have enough to get started—and you'll pick up whatever you need along the way if you keep going.

---

* I found this quote in an obscure book, *Acting in Film,* which Caine wrote in 1990. It's not a gossipy memoir, although it is endlessly charming and readable. It's about the nuts and bolts of performing in front of a camera, making an impression, and building a career—in other words, it is a primer on identity and reputation.

Second rule: Move quickly. One brick at a time isn't a license to go slowly. You're constructing a sequence of successes, and you might as well do it quickly. The smaller the gap between your serial achievements, the easier they are to notice. Also, there's a fine line between patience and procrastination. If you must err, err on the side of urgency. People pay attention to someone who's in a hurry.

Third rule: Say two no's for every yes. You never want to turn down a chance to get involved in something good, but in my experience, dead ends outnumber opportunities in almost any walk of life. For every good idea, there are dozens of bad ones. So be more ruthless about saying no, especially when other people try to steer you off course. When someone asks for help, unless it's inappropriate or thoughtless to say no, weigh every yes as if you were spending money. If it distracts you from your goal, don't do it—no matter how tempting the upside seems. Think of your reputation as a wall that you're building one brick at a time. If you're using red bricks and suddenly insert a yellow brick, the wall doesn't look right—and people notice. That's what saying yes to the wrong idea can do to the reputation you're trying to rebuild. You've broken your carefully constructed string of achievements—and sown confusion.

Fourth rule: It pays to advertise. I know a playwright who never reveals what new work she's writing. "When you talk about it," she says, "you're not writing it. You're just talking." That sort of secretiveness may apply to creative work, but it doesn't apply to rebuilding your reputation—and Mojo. People have preconceptions about you. They not only filter everything you do through those preconceptions, but they are constantly looking for evidence that confirms them. Thus, if they believe you are perennially late, even when you're only a few seconds late to a lunch date or a meeting, they'll quietly file that away as Exhibit #913 of your tardiness. However, if you tell them that you're making a serious effort to be on time from now on, that bit of "advertising" can dramatically change their perception of you. They'll be on the alert for evidence of your on-time behavior rather than confirmation that you're always late. That little tweak in perception, created solely by telling people that you're trying to change, can make all the difference.

TOOL #6:
Live Your Mission in the Small Moments Too

When Peter Drucker worked with an organization or an individual, he always posed five very basic questions. The first was: "What is your mission?"* Peter began with the premise that you cannot figure out where you're going or how to get there until you articulate what that destination looks like. Simple concept, but it's amazing to me how many people never articulate their "mission" to themselves or to anyone else.

I realize that mission statements are regarded now as overbaked relics of the 1980s—a faddish buzzword of the same vintage as "excellence" and "quality." That may be true, but the fact that a concept is no longer the newest fad does not mean it doesn't have value. What turned mission statements into a corporate joke was how quickly companies broadcast their embrace of a concept and then didn't follow up on it with consistent action. You don't *write* a mission statement. You live it and breathe it. A lot of organizations never did that.

So let's make a deal here. I won't ask you to broadcast your personal mission statement. I won't give you pointers on how to write it down. So much has been written about mission statements, I don't need to add to the literature here. I'll only ask you to consider what your mission is by asking: What do you want to achieve and how do you want to achieve it?

I can accept that many people are incapable of answering these two questions. What I can't accept is someone sitting in judgment of other people who have adequately answered these questions for themselves.

I met a relief worker in Africa who had boiled her personal mission down to two words: "To serve." This may seem too broadly generalized to some people, but she had narrowed down her way of "serving" to helping sick and starving children in Africa. After that, even though she was doing some of the most emotionally grueling and thankless work imaginable, she found it easy to justify her actions, her decisions, and her life. She filtered every choice by asking herself, "Am I being of service?"

---

* The four other questions were: Who is the customer? What does your customer consider value? What are your desired results? What is your plan?

Another one of my friends wants to "make as much money" as he can. He just likes making money. He gives a ton away to charity and does not live an opulent lifestyle. For him making money is fun and exciting.

Two different people. Two different missions. Both finding meaning and fulfillment in their work—both functioning with high Mojo.

When you have a mission, you give yourself a purpose—and that adds clarity to all the actions and decisions that follow.

There's an underestimated value to articulating your mission: It focuses you, points you in a new direction, alters your behavior, and as a result, changes other people's perception of you.

I have only one caveat. Once you define a mission, you have to act on it consistently, not selectively. It's easy to walk the talk at the big obvious moments—like giving speeches. Anyone but the most appalling hypocrite can do that. But we establish our mission and prove its value in the small moments more than in the big ones.

I learned this from my wonderful friend Frances Hesselbein when she was CEO of the Girl Scouts of America. Frances is a hero of mine, a woman of true wisdom who is Peter Drucker's equivalent in the nonprofit world. She's also a very effective leader. When she was the CEO of the Girl Scouts, her mission was an oft-repeated mantra: "We are here for only one reason: to help girls and young women reach their highest potential." One of the ways she interpreted that was by not allowing anything—not ego, not a sense of entitlement, not a need for recognition—to get in the way of helping girls and young women.

Years ago she asked if I would conduct a leadership training session for a gathering of her Major City chapter leaders at the Girl Scouts' conference center just north of New York City. As we were scheduling the sessions, I was having trouble making the dates work. My only open day was a Saturday.

Frances said, "You are a volunteer. If you are willing to work on a Saturday, we are willing to work on a Saturday."

I was embarrassed by what I had to say next. "Frances, this is awkward for me, but I'll have been on the road for more than a week before I see you. There's only so much I can carry with me. I'm going to need help with my laundry."

"No problem," she said. "We have laundry facilities at the conference center. Just pile up the dirty laundry on the floor of your room and we'll get it cleaned for you."

That Saturday morning, wearing my last clean shirt, I did as directed: I left a pile of clothes in the middle of my room, then joined several of the Girl Scout leaders down the hall, where they were having a light breakfast. As we were talking, one of the women looked up and nodded to a friend. I followed her gaze to where I, along with everyone else in the room, could see Frances walking down the hallway, carrying my dirty laundry. As the CEO, she could have asked anyone on her staff to handle this chore and they would have done it. But she did it herself.

Frances was just being herself. Without even thinking about it, she demonstrated leadership and her dedication to service. Her small, fleeting gesture was not missed by the women I was talking with.

The Girl Scouts is a nonprofit organization. Except for the executive staff, it's populated by volunteers whose mission is to serve girls. In handling my laundry herself, Frances was sending a clear message—this is how we help people who volunteer to help us. It's not about ego. The mission is more important than anyone's ego. In this small gesture with the laundry, she was reinforcing the mission in a big way, and it had a big impact on me. So big that twenty years later I still remember it, and if humanly possible, I will do just about anything Frances Hesselbein asks me to do.

Keep this in mind as you try to carry out your mission, whatever it may be. There will be little off-the-radar moments where you think you can relax. Don't do it. The so-called little moments are precisely when we reinforce the value of our mission in the biggest way. What are the "small" gestures that you can make—which are not really small at all?

TOOL #7:
Swim in the Blue Water

Judith was an apparel executive who was lured away from a good job to run a flagging division at a rival company. Her mandate was to restore her group to profitability. She had a five-year cushion to do this. Her challenge was not only taking over a moribund division, but standing out among the company's three other divisions who were direct competitors with minor niche differences. I caught up with Judith over lunch three years into her tenure, and she was beaming with success. Her division had introduced a hit product line that was the talk of the industry, delivering monster profits ahead of schedule and outpacing her three intra-corporate rivals. I asked her how she had done it. She told me:

"I couldn't compete for the same designers, the same materials, and the same customers as the other divisions. Those divisions were already established and the people running them were huge personalities. If I tried to swim in the same water with them, I'd get eaten alive. So instead of drowning in my own blood, I decided to venture out into the 'blue water' where no one else was competing—the uncontested space. I hired creative people from neglected places like Australia and eastern Europe. I identified a couple of underserved customer bases and went after them. And I placed big bets that, to my amazement, paid off big. But the key was that I didn't have a choice except to find the "blue water." Anything less and I'd sink before I could swim."*

Judith's contrarian strategy not only bolstered her identity (message: she wasn't like everyone else), but it changed the context of her achievements. She was not only contributing to the company's growth, but it was the best kind of growth—the kind that's unexpected. It was like having a start-up that turns a profit years ahead of projections.

I realize it's dangerous to extrapolate a personal strategy out of a corporate competitive strategy. We are human beings, not SBUs (strategic business units). But there's some appeal in the idea that we can find a "blue water" alternative as we shape our personal aspirations. If everyone we know is looking one way, it makes sense for us to consider another way.

The idea certainly applies to the achievements that form our identity and reputation—and in turn, our Mojo—especially if it teaches us to

---

* Alert readers might recognize the blue/red water metaphor from the 2005 bestseller *Blue Ocean Strategy*, by W. Chan Kim and Renee Mauborgne. In that book, two professors at INSEAD, France's leading business school, divided the marketing universe into *Red Oceans* (the known market space comprising all the markets in existence today), where companies outperform rivals by grabbing a greater share of existing demand, and *Blue Oceans* (the unknown market space, untainted by competition, comprising all the markets *not* in existence today), where demand is created rather than fought over and the growth potential is limited only by one's imagination. When I asked Judith if she was familiar with the book, she said no. She just liked the image of red water and its implicit warning to avoid swimming with killer sharks.

seek our opportunities and invest our personal resources in the neglected or uncontested areas of a business, where the competition is neither crowded nor stiff. In hindsight, Judith's strategy makes perfect sense (most achievements do in hindsight), but it took courage and insight for her to resist direct competition with her peers. Most of us, if we're honest with ourselves, want to be judged by how well we play on the same field with the same rules as everyone else. It's a natural competitive urge we develop in grade school, where none of us wants the stigma of being treated as "special." The smarter move, of course, is to suppress that blunt burst of ego—and seek a niche that's untapped and unclaimed. Would you rather be the number four player in a big pond (where the growth potential is restricted by competitors) or number one in a much smaller pond (where the growth potential is limitless)? There is no correct answer for that. But I know which one I'd choose—because early in my career, I made just such a choice.

If I'm known for any original ideas among human resource professionals, it is my "development" of customized 360-degree feedback. When I started in the 1980s, 360-feedback already had significant traction in the corporate world. But it occurred to me that not all companies were alike. They had different cultures and expectations of their employees. So why should their 360 programs be uniform? What if you tailored the feedback questions to an organization's specific needs? Incredibly, no one was asking that question or presenting the alternative to big corporations. So I did. I found my "blue water" in the middle of a red ocean, not beyond it. I didn't create a new market; I offered a "new and improved" product to the existing market. It was a safe niche that for a long time was mostly mine.

Successful people don't deny this impulse to differentiate themselves; they embrace it. The impulse doesn't have to appear in outsized form, where we think we have to reinvent the wheel in order to find our place in the world. Like my minor contribution to 360-feedback, it can be small in scope and ambition. It merely has to be yours—and yours alone. It can appear in all we do, in how we do our job, how we think, how we interact with others, even how we communicate.

I always remember this small scene in the Harrison Ford movie *Clear and Present Danger*, where the President of the United States convenes a group of advisers to deal with a crisis: One of the President's friends and major fund-raisers has been assassinated by Colombian drug dealers for whom he was laundering money. The press hasn't gotten hold of the story, but it will be a major scandal if they do. The President's chief advisers unanimously recommend that he put as much distance as possible between himself and his murdered money-laundering friend. If there's no relationship, there's no story. The press might not even pick up on it. The President has doubts that the press won't find out. "They will," he says. "They always do."

Bucking the prevailing groupthink in the room, CIA analyst Jack Ryan, played by (surprise!) Ford, suggests the opposite approach in handling the media: Don't cover up. Open up. "If they ask were you friends," he tells the President, "say, 'No, we were *good* friends.' If they ask were you close, say, 'We were *lifelong* friends.' Don't give them any room to go. End of story."

Then he adds his Zen-like coda, "There's no sense defusing a bomb after it has already gone off."

It's a screenwriter's surefire scene to establish that the hero Jack Ryan is not like everyone else—he zigs when others zag—and it immediately earns the President's trust.

Our identities and reputations are made in such small, incisive moments. We can't all be transformative geniuses who see the world in a paradigm-shifting light. We can't all be inventors of the PC in a mainframe world. But we can all find a way to differentiate ourselves, however minimally, from the thundering herd—and in doing so, we achieve a small slice of singularity in our world.

If you want to enhance your Mojo, you can do worse than pursue an achievement that has everyone wondering, *Why didn't I think of that?*

CHAPTER 14

Reputation:
Taking Control of Your "Story"

The tools in this chapter operate in that space where our identity and achievements intersect with the world—and shape our reputation. Tool #8 is a reminder that we control whether we choose to stay in a situation, or go. Tool #9 is about protecting our reputation in that fraught moment when we make our departure. Tool #10 helps us measure what we mistakenly believe is unmeasurable: how others see us. Tool #11 introduces a simple but valuable interpersonal diet.

TOOL #8:
When to Stay, When to Go

It's one of the toughest decisions we face in the workplace. Do we stay at our current job, or do we go?

I'm assuming (a) that the choice is up to you (i.e., you're not being forced out) and (b) that the new job you're considering is roughly equal to the one you're in now—that is, you're not running to a markedly better situation, one that pays better or offers more opportunities or is clearly more congenial with your lifestyle.

What makes it a tough decision is when the status quo is okay—neither so great (or you wouldn't be thinking of going) nor so miserable that bailing out is a no-brainer.

In those conditions, how do you make one of the most important decisions of your life? Sure, you can seek advice from other people, but let's be honest here. Even if you got unanimous feedback, the only opinion that matters in the end is your inner voice. But how do you know you're hearing that inner voice correctly?

This is where the Mojo Scorecard can work for you—because in distinguishing between our Professional and Personal Mojo, it clarifies what you need to change. It's either You (based on what you bring to the job) or It (based on what the job brings to you).

The higher you go and the closer you are to your "dream job," the more challenging this stay/go decision can seem. But when you're clear about what created the decision to stay or leave—was it something about You or was it the job (i.e., It)?—the decision often becomes obvious.

I remember some years ago when an acquaintance named Pierce was suddenly complaining about his job. I had never heard this kind of talk from Pierce, but what made it even more puzzling was that he was at the peak of his success. The year before he had pulled off a string of deal-making coups, and his CEO, in part to reward him but also to make sure he didn't jump to the competition, offered him a three-year contract, saying, "Think of a compensation package that will make you happy."

Open-checkbook offers like that don't come along every day, but Mojo was coursing through Pierce's arteries—and his CEO sensed it and wanted to retain it. In no time at all, Pierce worked out a contract that elevated him from the middle ranks to the upper echelons of a three-thousand-employee company. It also made him one of the company's twenty highest-paid people. If anyone had cause to be happy, it was Pierce. Life wasn't good. Life was great.

What Pierce could not have foreseen was the dramatic change in his CEO's attitude toward him. Suddenly he was front and center on the CEO's radar. This was a double-edged sword. On the one hand, he liked the face time with the boss. On the other hand, it meant that the CEO felt entitled to call him at all hours to question his priorities or follow up on petty details or make silly demands.

"It was as if he felt giving me everything I wanted gave him permission to torture me," said Pierce. "It was perverse."

After a year of feeling crowded by his CEO, what Pierce had regarded as his dream job had become a mixed blessing.

I hadn't conceived the Mojo Scorecard at the time (this was eight years ago), but I suspect that if Pierce had filled it out, it would have delivered an unequivocal verdict. Pierce's Professional Mojo—i.e., what he felt about the skills that he brought to the job—would still have been high. His abilities as a great dealmaker had not diminished. But his Personal Mojo—i.e., the rewards, meaning, and happiness that the job provided him—would have been low, largely due to the way his CEO was treating him.

That's the value of dividing your Mojo into Professional and Personal categories. No matter how high your score is one area, you can be derailed by your lowest score. And if you're experiencing low Mojo in what the job is bringing to you, then you might need to change the job.

Pierce was in an odd situation. His skills were intact, but the environment for employing his skills had deteriorated to the point that he felt he had to change jobs. He told the CEO that he was quitting.

That's when the CEO surprised him again, with another open-ended offer.

"I don't want you to leave," said the CEO. "What would make you happy?"

(In this case, Pierce's CEO was being very wise. He realized that even though Pierce was his subordinate, Pierce was the "decision maker" in this career choice. Rather than trying to play "the boss," the CEO went into "salesperson" mode and worked on influencing Pierce.)

Seizing the moment, Pierce gave a blunt response. "You have to get off my back and let me do my job," he said.

Until that moment, the CEO had had no idea that he had been "torturing" his star executive and making his work life untenable. The two men talked it out, the CEO promised to stop crowding Pierce, and Pierce decided to stay. He changed It (in this case, his situation) rather than himself. His CEO was wise enough to change himself (in this case, his need for control) rather than the situation.

When I began developing this book, one of the first people to use the Scorecard was a marketing executive I worked with named Teri. She had jumped from job to job in her twenties and early thirties, but she finally felt home at a health food company in Pennsylvania. Within five years, after she developed a hit product that delivered half the company's profits, she was named president of the most important division. She was earning a seven-figure salary—and she was miserable.

That's when I happened to meet Teri and had her give the Mojo Scorecard a trial run for a typical day. I wanted to pinpoint why she was unhappy in a job that, on paper, offered her everything she could ask for: authority,

Teri's Scorecard

THE MOJO SCORECARD

	ACTIVITY	PROFESSIONAL MOJO						PERSONAL MOJO						MOJO SCORE
		MOTIVATION	KNOWLEDGE	ABILITY	CONFIDENCE	AUTHENTICITY	TOTAL	HAPPINESS	REWARDS	MEANING	LEARNING	GRATITUDE	TOTAL	
1.	7:00 B'fast w/ CEO	10	9	9	9	9	46	8	8	8	9	9	42	88
2.	8:30 E-mails	4	8	8	6	4	30	3	2	1	2	2	10	40
3.	9:30 Conference call w/ vendor	8	9	9	9	9	44	6	4	5	6	4	25	69
4.	10:30 Packaging design meeting	10	10	10	9	9	48	6	4	5	6	4	25	73
5.	11:30 Phone calls	9	7	9	7	7	39	4	4	4	4	4	20	59
6.	12:30 In-house lunch w/ sales dis.	10	9	9	9	9	46	6	4	5	6	4	25	71
7.	1:30 E-mails	4	8	8	6	4	30	3	2	1	2	2	10	40
8.	2:00 Phone interview w. reporter	9	10	9	9	6	43	8	8	6	9	6	37	80
9.	3:00 Meeting w/ CFO	6	6	6	6	6	30	4	4	4	4	4	20	50
10.	4:00 Meeting w/ marketing staff	10	9	9	9	9	46	5	4	5	5	4	23	69
11.	5:00 Weekly division heads mtg.	9	9	9	9	8	44	6	5	6	5	4	26	70
12.	6:00 E-mails	3	7	7	5	3	25	2	2	1	2	2	9	34
13.	6:30 Conference call to West Coast	8	7	7	8	7	37	4	5	5	4	2	20	57

great pay, and the satisfaction of seeing her ideas ship out the door and succeed in the marketplace. Was it the job that had changed, or was it Teri?

I was hoping Teri's Scorecard would provide the answer.

Her Professional Mojo was high, which wasn't surprising. Teri was a
very capable and motivated executive; she brought a lot to any task, and it
showed in how she rated herself on motivation, knowledge, ability (or
skills), confidence, and authenticity.

Her Personal Mojo, however, was spotty, confirming that she was
finding neither happiness nor meaning in much of what she did all day.
Note how low her scores are during her daily staff meeting with her de-
partment heads. When I asked Teri about this, she explained that she felt
powerless when her staff brought up problems that needed fixing—not
because she couldn't handle them, but because she had no confidence her
staff would resolve them to her satisfaction.

It was a common problem that I'd seen many times before when capable hands-on people are promoted to senior leadership positions. Suddenly they don't have enough time to sink their hands into every niggling
problem. They have to rely on others and *hope* these people do their jobs
well. They lose control at the precise moment when they acquire power.

"Your job has changed," I told her. "You're the boss now. You can't fix
everything yourself and it's killing your Mojo."

Teri was unhappy at work, feeling trapped in a big job that she couldn't
tailor to provide happiness and meaning. Since she couldn't change the
job, she decided to change who she was. She would change herself from a
corporate leader who had to rely on others to a solo practitioner who only
had to rely on herself. That meant quitting her job and starting up her
own operation in the same field: healthy foods. On day one, she had one
employee—herself. But she was happy with that.

I like to think that the Mojo Scorecard helped Teri identify the
source of her unhappiness. It wasn't that she couldn't satisfy the job's
requirements. It was that the job that couldn't satisfy hers.

Jim in another company had almost an identical problem to Teri's,
but chose the opposite response—with an equally positive outcome. Jim
changed himself. He realized that being a great leader, which he wanted
to be, meant learning how to delegate effectively and empower others. He
admitted that much of the problem was him—not his team members. He

recruited his team to help him become a great delegator and, guess what, he succeeded!

Teri and Jim chose totally different approaches to solving the same problem. Neither approach was "better" or "worse." Both worked. Teri changed the situation, and Jim changed himself.

No one can tell you which approach is better for you. My advice is simple: Consider your long-term Mojo. Can you find more happiness and meaning by changing the situation? Can you find more happiness and meaning by changing yourself? What are your real alternatives?

Conduct a Mojo analysis—make your decision—accept the trade-offs—and get on with life.

TOOL #9:
Hello, Good-bye

We all know that how we arrive at a new job is a good predictor of how we will be received in that job. That's why we're so careful to put our best foot forward in our first days in a new situation. We're alert to how early we show up at the office and how late we stay. We're a little more cautious about how we speak to our new colleagues, not wishing to rub people the wrong way. We act with one eye on our actual job and the other eye on the impression we're making. Much of this self-consciousness fades in a few weeks, as we find our bearings, settle into a routine, and become our more "natural" selves. But our success is more likely if we make a heroic effort at the start.

If only people paid as much attention to their departure as they do to their arrival.

Few events create more immediate damage to your Mojo than having to depart from a job that you love. Sometimes the departure comes in the form of a brutal firing. Sometimes you're part of the crowd in a mass layoff. Sometimes it's a slow death, through a demotion or a shrinkage of your power base. Sometimes you're squeezed out because you don't have anything to do. Whatever the cause of a departure, it's not only the dings and bruises to your psyche that you have to account for, but also the potential damage to your reputation. No matter how you dress up a dismissal—whether it's the vague "I'm leaving to pursue other interests" or the comically euphemistic "I want to spend more time with my family"—you still have to deal with the perception that something went wrong, you came up short, and you may not be all that you're cracked up to be.

But it doesn't have to be quite that bad, not if you employ one or more of these exit strategies:

1. Have a Pre-Exit Strategy

It's a commonplace in leadership thinking that when an employee is surprised about getting fired, the surprise is management's fault. Either the boss didn't train the employee well or didn't provide adequate warning via reviews. While that may be true, I think the employee can also shoulder some of the responsibility. Given all the anxiety that employees feel about job security (in the down economy of 2009, 47 percent of polled workers said they worried "a lot" or "some" about losing their jobs), there's no excuse for not seeing bad news coming or not being prepared for the worst. Here's a tool, in the form of a chart, that can help.

Basically, when we take our leave of a job, we do it under two types of locomotion: either we jump or we are pushed. And we do it either on our way up or on our way down. These forces—jump vs. push, up vs. down—create an interesting dynamic that lays out our options when we're feeling less than secure at work.

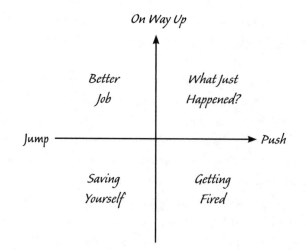

The vertical line in this matrix tracks how you're perceived at work. It's your honest assessment of whether you are riding a wave of success or feel that you've fallen behind. Is your career trajectory pointing up or down? The horizontal line lays out your options. Leaving a job is either your choice or someone else's. The resulting four quadrants identify the reasons behind most departures from a job. Which quadrant do you belong in?

Hopefully, you place yourself above the horizontal line, not below it (and certainly not in the lower-right quadrant, where you're not performing well and everyone knows it). You want your career to be in ascendance. That means you're desirable to other employers. It means you have the option to jump to a better job. But don't be fooled: It's no guarantee that you're invulnerable. I've seen a few unfortunate cases where great people were unfairly squeezed out of their jobs precisely because they were on the way up and were perceived as a threat to their alleged "superiors." It also happens frequently after a merger or acquisition when redundancies in the merged operations send many capable people packing. If you suspect you're in this quadrant—in danger of getting pushed out when you're at the top of your game—you need an honest appraisal of how secure your boss feels about his or her job. Are you considered an asset or a threat? If you are part of a merger, does the new organization recognize your talent?

The lower-left quadrant may be the trickiest to negotiate. You're not doing well (in the eyes of the company), so you jump before you get pushed out. Of course, you have to have something to jump to. The key factor here is appreciating that even though you're down in your company's eyes, the rest of the world may not have caught up to that fact. That discrepancy between your reputation inside the company and outside is a "market anomaly" that can work to your advantage. But you have to act swiftly. The window doesn't stay open forever.

A key element in protecting your reputation is taking "preventative medicine" to ensure it doesn't get damaged.

Deciding whether to stay in an organization or go is usually tough. Deciding to "jump" rather than be "pushed out" is easy!

2. The Three Envelopes

The new CEO of a high-tech company was going through a tough year. Sales and profits were down. Although he was very worried about his company, he wasn't very worried about having a job.

When I asked him why he wasn't worried about losing his job, he said, "I just got here. The Board is at least going to give me a chance."

He then told me a classic joke that the previous CEO had told him.

"A new CEO met privately with his predecessor on his first day in charge. The CEO who was stepping down presented him with three numbered envelopes. 'Open these—one at a time—and only when you run up against a crisis that seems beyond your control,' he said.

"Things went along pretty smoothly, but six months later, sales took a downturn and he was catching a lot of heat. He remembered the envelopes. He went to his drawer and took out the first envelope. The message read, 'Blame the previous CEO!'

"The new CEO called a press conference and tactfully laid the blame at the feet of the previous CEO. Satisfied with his comments, the media and Wall Street responded positively, sales began to pick up, and the problem was soon behind him.

"A couple of years later, the company was hit again with a dip in sales combined with serious product problems. The CEO thought, 'Aha! Time for envelope two!' The CEO opened the second envelope. The message read, 'Blame the economy!' Times were tough for everyone in the industry. This seemed to work fine. He was ready for another business cycle.

"After several consecutive profitable quarters, the company once again fell on difficult times. The CEO closed his office door and opened the third envelope.

"The message said, 'Prepare three envelopes!'

"You see, Marshall," he concluded. "I'm on my first envelope."

I'd heard the joke before, but it's a great reminder to all of us that we shouldn't panic after our first setback. The world can be tough and competitive, but more often than not, it's also at least a little forgiving.

The challenge for today's world is that your "three envelopes" may get used up faster than ever before. Even at the CEO level, "time in grade" is going down.

My career advice is simple. Do your best to "read the tea leaves." Don't panic when you are new, yet don't get lost in your own ego. It can be tough out there. If you think your time may be coming to an end, it probably is. Leave the company (on positive terms)—before the company leaves you (on negative terms).

3. Stop the Identity Theft

When I talked to people on Wall Street during the upheavals of 2008 and 2009, I was startled to find that what upset many laid-off employees was not the loss of personal income or the sense of betrayal by their bosses or the blunt fact that they didn't have a job anymore. Yes, those were powerful consequences of losing a job. But the biggest hurt for many people was the loss of a clear identity. Their jobs at firms like the now-defunct Lehman Brothers or Bear Stearns were the badges that announced who they were. Without the job, they felt unmoored, confused, unsure who they really were. As one unemployed banker told me, "I feel like a victim of identity theft."

This was startling to me because, with all the media stories about how we're an economy of "free agents" hopscotching from job to job selling our services to the highest bidder, it's easy to forget that the majority of people in the workforce *don't* think of themselves as free agents. They like the idea of being rooted to one company, and that's borne out by statistics. The average length of an American worker's stay at one company is still thirteen years.

I don't have an immediate cure for this sense of lost identity. Whatever I say would be as futile as telling a lovesick son who's just broken up with his girlfriend, "Suck it up. You'll get over it." While the statement may be true, it doesn't provide any healing to a raw wound.

The best advice I can offer is this: Accept that your identification with your vanished job is pointless, and move quickly to transfer your affections to something else. It might be a new job, if you're lucky enough to find one. It might be a start-up business, providing you with the wholly new identity of "entrepreneur." But it could also be volunteer work, or devoting yourself in your downtime to a new hobby or a revived fitness regimen. Anything is better than bitterness, anger, or pining for old times that are not coming back.

When you look for a new position, focus on what you can contribute to the new firm—not just what you did at the old firm. If your old firm failed, be prepared for the possibility of "moving down"—at least in the short-term. If you get your Mojo back, and prove what you can do in the new firm, you can get back to where you were. If you believe that you can start at where you were, you might end up with nothing.

4. How Much of Your Reputation Is Really Yours?

The flip side of having your identity so indelibly linked to your job is over-estimating how much of your good standing among people is due to who you are rather than who you work for. It's a common error. When we work for a first-rate organization with enormous prestige in its industry, much of that prestige automatically attaches to us simply because we can say we work there. But it's not really our prestige—and it's not permanent. It can disappear the moment we leave the organization. It's amazing to me how many otherwise smart and accomplished people don't appreciate this.

One of my friends found this out the hard way when he left one of the world's most prestigious consulting firms—by his own choice—and started his own consulting business.

I have personally had a "guaranteed base salary" of zero for over thirty years. I know what it is like to live outside of a big-company environment. While I am used to this life, and love it, I know how tough it can be for many people who are used to collecting a check every month. I tried to caution my friend on the difference between "being your own brand" and "being part of a corporate brand." He didn't listen very well.

When my friend left the consulting firm he had a few "transition" clients that left with him, but these short-term projects ended in a few months. He quickly found out that corporate purchasers were much more likely to spend money on "name" firms than on untested individuals.

My friend's problems were partially caused by his own ego. His big firm's clients were very nice to him and kept telling him what a great job he was doing. He developed an "I don't need you" attitude toward his large, respected firm. When he left, he was a little too "cocky." He was pretty disrespectful to the partners in the firm and not very thankful for all that they had done to help him become a success.

He then proceeded to overprice himself and was too proud to lower his prices when his business started drying up. He eventually had to swallow his pride and is back at work in another large firm—only at a much lower level and making a lot less money.

In his case, he changed "It" when he should have changed "You."

Keep this in mind when you plan a hasty or angry departure—and you currently have a good job. Ask yourself: How solid is my reputation? And is it solid because of what I've done or who I work for? The answer can make all the difference.

TOOL #10:
Adopt a Metrics System

One of the inspirations for this book came from a discussion I had a few years ago with a financial adviser named Martin. Martin handled investments for high-net-worth individuals, where the minimum account was $5 million. He was good at his job, taking home a seven-figure salary most years. Although that was a lot less than most of his clients earned annually, it didn't bother Martin. He lived and breathed investing, and he adored his clients, many of whom were self-made entrepreneurs and CEOs. Martin enjoyed talking with them on the phone or advising them personally over expensive meals. It was his favorite part of the job. Martin built up his client list by beating the market regularly, but also through word-of-mouth from his first big CEO client, who recommended Martin to his friends at every opportunity. This is how success happens: a lot of know-how abetted by a little know-who.

One day Martin was informed by a curt e-mail that the CEO was leaving him. Martin thought it was because he'd failed to get along with the CEO's new wife. The CEO's e-mail read: "You don't seem to be as interested in us anymore."

Martin took the loss hard for a while. But he didn't think it would affect his business.

And for a few months it didn't. But then Martin noticed that many of the clients who had come to him via the CEO were trimming the size of their accounts with him. They said they were "diversifying," but the pattern (to a fellow like Martin who made his living analyzing figures and trends) was hard to ignore. The proof was a more personal metric. Martin noticed that he wasn't having as many face-to-face meetings or meals with some of his clients. Even worse, while there was a time when his busy clients used to drop everything to take his phone calls, now it was difficult getting through to them—and when he did, the conversations were no longer freewheeling and intimate; they were short and all business. Martin tested his suspicion over a few months by tracking how many calls he had to place to reach a client. He tracked the time it took to get his calls returned, as well as the time he spent on the phone. He accumulated elaborate data, which confirmed his fears.

"It's as if I have body odor," he told me. "I've lost my Mojo."

Martin wasn't using the term "Mojo" in quite the same way as our operational definition in this book, but he was close. If Mojo is the "juice" that puts the spring in your step at work—and that everyone responds to positively—then his metrics suggested he was losing some of it. Clients were avoiding him.

What interested me more than his Mojo, however, was Martin's use of a personal metric to deal with a problem. He not only measured his phone activity to confirm a hunch but *he used it to confirm something negative.*

A personal metric is any set of data or information that we assemble to help us understand a situation. Customarily we think of "metrics" as numbers that explain the state of our business affairs—hard data for traditional measurements like cash flow, market share, revenue growth, employee retention rates, return on investment, and so on. Personal metrics are warmer and fuzzier data, coming into play when we need to understand emotions and feelings and relationships.* We don't usually apply numbers to these aspects of our lives, or at least it's not as easy to do and therefore not as common. But we should. That's what Martin was doing

---

* One of my favorite "emotional interpretations" of a common metric is reporter Jeff Coplon's analysis of the New York Knicks' lowly status in 2008. The team ranked dead last in assists and averaged the fewest blocked shots since the NBA started keeping the stat. "In short," wrote Coplon, "they neither shared nor cared."

when he analyzed his phone calls. It wasn't hard data about profits and losses. It was "soft" information, and yet given his client problems, it was the most valuable metric he could have employed at that moment in time.

We all employ personal metrics to measure our progress during the day. If we're on a diet, our metric is stepping on the bathroom scale each morning. If we're trying to quit smoking, we'll count the number of cigarettes we light up each day. If we're training for a marathon, we'll track our weekly mileage. If a number can be attached to it, we'll measure it.*

The most pervasive metric, of course, involves money: how much of it we're earning, how much we've saved, how much others are earning, and so on. We're always measuring money.

But here's the thing about how we use our private metrics. We love the data when they deliver good news. We ignore them when the news is not to our liking. That's the reason that during the boom years from 2004 to 2007, so many people enjoyed checking the value of their stock portfolios online three or four times a day (a rising market lifts all quotes). But after market indexes fell 30 to 50 percent across the board in 2008, the frequency of civilian investors going online to check their portfolios dropped significantly.

This isn't surprising behavior. If our bathroom scale reads out disappointing numbers, we'll stop getting on the scale. Giving up on metrics is always a part of giving up on change.

What I'd like to suggest here is that measuring the "bad numbers" is precisely what we need to do more often. Measuring only positive progress is like surrounding ourselves with sycophants: good for the ego perhaps, but not the most accurate picture of how we're doing. Applying personal metrics when the numbers may be depressing not only tells us where we're failing but also how to change our luck.

Take Martin. It took imagination and guts to analyze his phone activity to determine that his emotional bond with clients was fraying: imagination because he was trying to quantify people's feelings without asking

---

* I knew one data-obsessed entrepreneur who kept track of how many hours he slept each night. I'm not sure what comfort the numbers provided when he added them up at year's end. His wife had the best explanation: "He achieves rest," she said.

them directly (which is not easy to do) and guts because the results could be painful. But once he saw the data, he knew how to confront his falling Mojo head on. He called clients and asked, "Is something wrong?" And they said yes. The CEO who sacked Martin was telling the truth: He left because of Martin's waning "interest." As Martin's client list grew, he had spread himself too thin, and his original clients, accustomed to Martin's heavy personal touch, felt neglected. Hearing this, Martin promised to do better, trimming his list to a more manageable size by off-loading newer clients to colleagues. His relationship with clients was more important to him than generating more fees. Without applying his personal metric, however, he'd never have learned that.

The obvious value of personal metrics is that they give us concrete feedback in areas where we usually rely on hunches, impressions, and casual scraps of evidence. For example, let's say as a parent you feel a disconnect with your teenage children. You decide to analyze your relationship with them by counting the number of times they initiate a conversation with you. A friend of mine did this over the course of two months and discovered that his children rarely talked to him unless he said something first. Conclusion: He had serious mending to do with his kids. He had sort of suspected it (hence, the test), but he didn't know it for sure until he gathered the data.

But the real beauty of our personal metrics is that not only may they reveal a painful truth that we're avoiding, but they can also provide us with a portal of entry into a delicate subject. With numbers in hand, we can broach any topic. Sometimes they allow us to confront a tough situation without being confrontational.

To make a personal metric a key part of your Mojo Tool Kit, begin by asking yourself what "bad news" is affecting your Mojo. Then ask yourself whether you're avoiding it or willing to confront it.

It might be a feeling that you're wasting too much of your time at work on fruitless tasks. It might be a hunch that a client isn't totally in your corner anymore. It might be a sense that you've become mal-employed at work—that you're being assigned tasks not totally congenial to your talents. Suspicions like these can always be measured with disciplined observation and tracking—much in the same way that Martin tracked how quickly his clients jumped off the phone with him or my neighbor measured how often his kids started a conversation. Once you have your personal metric, no matter how alarming the data, you'll know what to do next. The only question you have to deal with now is: What's holding you back?

TOOL #11:
Reduce This Number

Here's a personal metric that you may not have measured for yourself, but which I find revealing because I think it is one of the major causes of Mojo loss in the workplace. It involves how much of our interpersonal communication is spent on pointless, nonproductive topics. I will be amazed (and skeptical) if you think it does not somehow apply to you—or at least some of the members of your team.

Over the years I have asked thousands of participants in my classes to answer the following question: What percent of all interpersonal communication time is spent on (a) people talking about how smart, special, or wonderful they are—or listening while someone else does this, plus (b) people talking about how stupid, inept, or bad someone else is—or listening while someone else does this?

I then ask my "research subjects" to add up (a) and (b) for the percentage of their interpersonal communication that's spent on boasting, criticizing, or listening to this. There's no "correct" answer. I'm just looking for people's subjective guesses about the nature of communicating that goes on around them or that they participate in.

I've had some people estimate 100 percent, because they cynically believe all workplace communication serves only two purposes: either to build ourselves up or tear someone else down. They have a point, but it can't be *all* that people talk about. It's my job to look out for evidence of ego in the workplace, and I'm certainly not that cynical.

I've also received lowball estimates from 5 to 10 percent, no doubt offered by naïve shut-ins who never exchange gossipy e-mails, hang around the watercooler, or stay out late with coworkers.

When I toss out the high and low extremes, the final tally (with a consistency that has persisted over the years that I've been asking the question) is still astonishing to me. The average number is 65 percent.

In other words, according to thousands of respondents from around the world, two-thirds of the "stuff" we discuss with our coworkers involves either boasting or criticizing, by us or someone else.

What most makes this astonishing, of course, is the sheer pointlessness of all this chatter.

After all, when we talk about how smart, special, or wonderful we are, we learn nothing. When we talk about how stupid, inept, or bad someone else is, we learn nothing. When we listen while someone else does this, we learn nothing. If there were a prize for pointless behavior in the workplace, this would clinch it.

This 65 percent has become one of my pet metrics over the years, because it addresses an issue that most of us tend to ignore: how much productivity we lose each day in meaningless or destructive communication. I'm not talking about the everyday e-mails and memos and phone tag that already put a serious dent in our productivity. They're annoying, but harmless. The communication I'm referring to here has a distinct and specific quality; it's either poisonous or drenched in ego. Neither is good for your Mojo.

So here is the easiest-to-do productivity tool you'll find in this book. It costs nothing, it will save you time, and it will make your work and home life more positive: *Reduce this number.*

CHAPTER 15

Acceptance:
Change What You Can,
Let Go of What You Can't

The tools in this chapter will help you deal with some elements of life that you may not be able to directly control. Tool #12 shows how to more effectively influence your manager. Tool #13 explains how to better understand a situation by giving it a name. Tool #14 teaches the power of forgiveness.

TOOL #12:
Influence Up as Well as Down

In 2008 I was coaching a pharmaceutical CEO named Daniel when I noticed that every time the discussion turned to his Executive Vice President of Sales, Matt, Daniel's voice grew steely and cold. It was so obvious; it would have been malpractice for me to ignore it.

"Tell me about this fellow Matt," I said. "What's your opinion of him?"

"He's my best salesperson and the biggest pain in my butt," Daniel said. "He's arrogant and unmanageable. Here's a guy who should be my successor and I'm this close"—he spread his thumb and index finger an inch apart—"to kicking him out."

"It sounds like I should be working with him before you," I said.

"That's not a bad idea," said Daniel. And with that hint of a marching order, I paid a visit to Matt. Based on Daniel's description, I prepared myself to deal with a loud, angry, hyper-achieving ogre who would try to shoo me out of his office as quickly as he could. But Matt was one of the more disarming people I've ever met. He was smart, good-looking, athletic, and unfailingly polite. He didn't resent my visit. As I laid out the purpose of my call—namely, to tell him that he had a serious disconnect with his boss—he didn't automatically go into denial and dismiss the message or start arguing with me (as I had seen many other people do before). He seemed sincerely interested in understanding the problem.

As I left his office after that initial meeting, I was puzzled. Matt appeared to be the total executive package. So, why the conflict with his boss? The answer came a couple of weeks later, after I assembled the feedback from Matt's colleagues and direct reports. His assistant Laurie summed it up succinctly.

"Matt's the best," she said. "The best at everything. Being a salesman, a leader, a boss, a pal. Everybody who reports to him loves him and everybody thinks he's dumb."

The last part startled me. "What makes him dumb?" I asked.

"He won't acknowledge that Daniel is the CEO," she said.

It was an acute insight—and instantly explained the conflict between two otherwise ideal executives.

Matt was guilty of Mojo Killer #3—looking for logic in all the wrong places—or at least a variation thereof. In his case, he couldn't get over the illogic or unfairness that a great salesperson like him had to obey decisions by a CEO like Daniel, who came out of finance and who (Matt believed) had no idea what it took to make the cash registers ring. Matt was expressing an emotion held by millions of "knowledge workers" in modern organizations. Knowledge workers are people who, because of their years of education and training, know more about what they're doing than their managers do. The stereotype is the cubicle-dwelling software programmer at a high-tech company—the Dilbert character—who knows more about writing code than the CEO, and resents the world for not recognizing how smart he is. But it could be any highly skilled specialist who feels superior to or unappreciated by the "generalist" above him or her.

Matt's case added an interesting irony to the scenario. He was a salesman, a master at influencing people. But he had neglected to apply his skills to influencing the most important person in his organizational life: Daniel, his boss. That's what his assistant Laurie meant by calling him "dumb."

The next time I met with Matt, I didn't sugarcoat the feedback. "Everybody who reports to you loves you—and everybody thinks you're an idiot," I said.

To his credit, Matt said, "Thank you." I don't usually get that reaction when I tell people they're seen as idiots. I get expressions of outrage. I get denials. I get excuses. I get arguments about why "everybody" is wrong. But it was another sign of Matt's sterling qualities that he expressed gratitude for the information. That's when I knew that Matt would be a very easy leader to help.

Feeling like a doctor writing a prescription, I scribbled the following on a notepad and told Matt to memorize it:

Every decision in the world is made by the person who has the power to make that decision—not the "right" person, or the "smartest" person, or the "most qualified" person, and in most cases not *you*. If you influence this decision maker, you will make a positive difference. If you do not influence this person, you will not make a positive difference. Make peace with this. You will have a better life! And, you will make more of a positive difference in your organization and you will be happier.

"You're talking about Daniel, aren't you?" said Matt, after struggling to decipher my handwriting.

You think?

"Look Matt," I said, "you've got great sales skills. But you don't treat Daniel the way you treat your customers. You argue with him. You resent him. And you don't hide your feelings very well. This is stupid. If Daniel were a customer, what would he do with you?"

"He'd throw me out of the building."

"You're right. He's this close to doing that. But you already know what to do. Start treating your boss like a customer. Focus on influencing up the same positive way you focus on influencing down."

And with that small insight, Matt immediately began to apply his salesman's instincts to repairing his relationship with his CEO. He did all the things a salesman does. He called back promptly. He followed up on the outcome of any action. He scheduled a face-to-face meeting or lunch every few weeks. And he didn't blame the customer for not buying what he was selling; after a normal discussion, if Daniel didn't go along with Matt's final decision, he accepted it. He didn't whine about the CEO's decision. He moved on.

Most behavioral changes take months to make an impression, but in this case the impact was evident in a matter of weeks (perhaps because the dysfunction was so acutely top-of-mind and involved only two people; in other words, the two parties were paying close attention). "I don't know what you said to Matt," Daniel told me, "but he's a different person."

Among the five most important questions that Peter Drucker posed to solve any management problem, the second and third are, "Who is the customer?" and "What does the customer value?" That's what Matt forgot. His CEO was clearly one of his important customers—and Matt clearly was not treating him that way.

It's a simple lesson, but that doesn't make it easy to remember or accept. We're guilty of it whenever we moan about a decision that's gone against us. We're moaning about our powerlessness rather than facing up to the reality of the situation. Oddly, the feeling doesn't go away as our authority increases. In many cases it becomes more virulent. That's the paradox I was driving into Matt. The higher you climb up the ladder and the closer you approach the pinnacle of power, the more tempted you may be to resent others who have even more power than you.

In a way, it makes perfect sense. Let's say over the course of time you ascend from middle management to a position where you're commanding an organization's most important or profitable division. The CEO's power has not diminished. But your power within the organization has dramatically increased. Every day, as you flex your authority over your team, you get more evidence that you are closer to being the CEO's peer rather than his or her subordinate. It's a perfectly natural feeling, but a dangerous one if it pumps up your self-regard to the point where you have delusions of grandeur and neglect the care and feeding of one of your most important customers, the boss.

I am not recommending a new-level sycophancy here. Being a "yes man" or "suck up" is rarely an effective long-term strategy. What I'm suggesting is that you should neither take your manager for granted nor resent his or her position as your boss. In every transaction, there's a buyer and a seller, a vendor and a customer. It's the same in the interpersonal transactions you conduct every day with your manager. In many interactions, you're the supplier; your manager is the customer. The moment you learn to accept that, everything changes for the better.

If you are leading people, you will not only be helping yourself, you will be helping them. Leaders who can sell and effectively "influence up" are much more likely to get the resources and support that their direct reports need for successful goal achievement. You will also be teaching your direct reports, by example, an important lesson—do what you can to achieve the mission and make a positive difference; don't get lost in your own ego.

TOOL #13:
Name It, Frame It, Claim It

If you want to improve your understanding of a situation, give it a name.

Naming something—whether it's a strategy we want to employ, or a tactic employed against us, or a colleague's behavior that catches us off guard, or a life-changing decision we have to make—lets us organize the action into a coherent shape. It lets us compare the action to what has gone before. It helps us retain it for future purposes, so that we may recognize—and respond to—the action more brilliantly the next time we face it. Naming helps us learn, make sense, and take control.

Most of us already engage in this kind of naming, whether we know it or not, with people and events that confront us every day. When we find ourselves in a meeting where everyone is ducking responsibility for a mistake and refer to it later as a "blame-storming session," we're framing an *event* as a waste of time. When we employ a nickname based on a colleague's performance ("The Closer") or physical characteristic ("Red"), either sincerely or ironically, we're using the nickname to frame and focus what an *individual* means to us.* As parents, when we see our kids going to our spouse seeking permission for something that we have already denied, we have a name for that tactic: "divide and conquer." It reminds us not to fall for this trap and that a united front will stop it cold.

---

* In this context my favorite sports nickname is "Mr. October," which attached itself to New York Yankees slugger Reggie Jackson in recognition of his repeat heroics in baseball's postseason. It was so pithy and vivid, it inspired Yankees owner George Steinbrenner to sarcastically nickname another high-priced slugger "Mr. May" in honor of his lackluster hitting when it really mattered, in the postseason.

In that sense, naming is not much different than running into someone vaguely familiar to us on the street or at a party. The face registers, but we cannot recall the person's name. If we hang around long enough, eventually the name comes back to us—or the person sees our confusion and tells us his or her name. That's the moment when our recognition and memory immediately improve. We say, "Of course!" as we mentally associate that name with other names, which creates vivid mental pictures of when and where we saw this person last. Slowly, we remember why we know him or her, who introduced us, what we talked about, what we have in common, whether we like the person and looked forward to running into each other again. A well-stocked packet of information is delivered to our brain for processing through the simple vehicle of hearing the person's name.

Imagine if you could attach a name to every aggressive or threatening or deceptive tactic you had to deal with in the workplace or in your civilian life. For example, a local merchant lures you into a store by advertising a ridiculously low price for a much-wanted item. When you get to the store, however, you are informed that the item is "sold out." If you are reasonably alert, experienced, and suspicious, you will recognize that you've been sucker-punched by one of the oldest sales tricks in the merchant's repertoire, the venerable and despicable "bait and switch." Just saying the name to yourself puts you on high alert and in a combative mood. It instantly brings up all your past experiences with similar tactics by similar people. You know exactly how to respond, almost without thinking.

I realize that, in one sense, naming is as commonplace as the air we breathe. That's particularly true in professions such as medicine, the law, finance, and sports, which would all be incomprehensible without their jargon. Jargon is just another name for prefabricated naming. Its job is the same: to frame a situation in a new light so we can recognize it and deal with it.

Consider the word "sack" in football. It refers to a defensive play where the quarterback is tackled behind the line of scrimmage with the ball. It doesn't happen too often, maybe three or four times a game. Its rarity alone makes it important. But it has great tactical significance because it not only pushes the offensive team backward, but physically punishes the quarterback, which could make him less effective later in the game.

Where did the word come from? Was it a reference to the sacking of cities by invading hordes in ancient times? Was it made up? Was it adopted simply because it sounded right?

It turns out that the word "sack" didn't exist in football before the mid-1960s. Who invented it is unknown. The National Football League didn't begin keeping statistics on sacks until 1982. And yet players had been tackling the quarterback behind the line of scrimmage for nearly a hundred years. Why did it take so many decades of football before someone attached a name to what was apparently one of the more important defensive achievements during a game?

The only answer I could come up with was that someone thought it was a crucial facet of the game, and naming it announced its importance. It added a new twist to the game, enhancing its complexity and, therefore, its interest to the public. It made you see in a new light something that was previously invisible or irrelevant. It also made you slightly smarter about the game of football. That's what the invention of the "sack" accomplished. Eventually, coaches came to regard the sack as one of those killer statistics that could almost predict the outcome of a game. The team with the numerical advantage in sacks is more likely to win. In one well-argued analysis, each sack was deemed to be theoretically worth three points to the team achieving it. Thus, a team with three sacks would have, say, a nine-point edge (in theory) over a team with none.

But none of this registered until someone gave the violent but noble pursuit of the quarterback a name.

What I'm suggesting here is that all of us could be a little more imaginative in how we name things—and it would dramatically improve our understanding of the world around us. At the risk of sounding like a Creativity 101 exercise, I suggest that for one day or for a whole week, you try this: Assign a name to every meaningful activity you do and every person that comes your way. If you commute by train to work each day, name the train. If you grab a cup of coffee before work, give the cup a name. If you have a meeting every Tuesday at 10:30 A.M., name it. If there's one colleague with whom you particularly enjoy working, name him or her. Same thing with a colleague who annoys you: Give the pest a nickname. It's an exercise in observation and judgment. How aware

are you of all that's going on around you? And what do you really think about it?*

I saw this with my client Miles, a seemingly cool and calm marketing executive whose big interpersonal issue was anger management. This was a surprise when I first met Miles, because he had a laid-back demeanor that suggested no person or situation could get under his skin. The feedback told a different story. Miles was easily frustrated with subordinates who didn't do their jobs properly. Rather than correct them with instructive leadership, he berated and abused them.

I asked Miles to pinpoint some examples in his daily routine when he felt low Mojo, when he was unhappy or frustrated. Miles quickly rattled them off. He got angry with his kid's soccer coach, who he thought didn't know what he was doing. He argued with his banker for overcharging a service fee. He even got into a shouting match with a clerk at an ice cream shop because he felt a hand-packed pint of vanilla was a couple of scoops short of a pint.

"Why do you care?" I finally asked, after hearing about the confrontation over ice cream. "It can't be that this store clerk cheated you out of fifty cents of ice cream. It's something besides money."

Although the examples he gave were incredibly trivial on the surface, they had a common theme, and I wanted Miles to see the pattern himself. It was a big one. Miles's low-Mojo moments arose when he felt frustrated— and what frustrated him was having to rely on people he felt were his inferiors. He thought he knew more about soccer than his kid's coach. He thought his banker was sloppy. He thought the ice cream server was lazy. This distaste for depending on people he didn't respect wasn't only manifest at work with his subordinates. It popped up in every part of his life.

"You're telling me I have a Superiority Complex," he said.

I was pleased that he named it himself. It meant he understood himself a little better.

---

* I tried this myself with a typical Monday in my life. The pre-dawn ride to the airport, which I've done a thousand times, was The Take Off. The flight itself, which is usually relaxing for me, was The Spa. The talk I gave to a room of over one thousand enthusiastic executives, which was the purpose of my trip, was Showtime. And so on. Okay, they're not very clever names. But do they succinctly express my attitude—and my Mojo—about each activity? Do they teach me something about how I'm living my life and where I could use improvement? Yes.

"That's right," I said. "It's your Achilles' heel. It triggers an unattractive side of you that's not only affecting the people under you, but poisoning your effectiveness as a boss. Now you have to remember that phrase. It's your Achilles' heel. Whenever you feel yourself getting angry at someone because you depend on them, just call up this name, 'Superiority Complex.' If it reminds you that it's an ugly side of you, maybe it will make you think twice about blowing up again."

Naming not only provides us with some private understanding of a situation that we keep to ourselves. We can also share the names we give things, so it has the potential to part the clouds of darkness for others as well.

One of my neighbors is one half of a successful songwriting team. The two men don't write hit songs that you download onto your iPod. They're not successful in that pop star sort of way. They write jingles and themes for commercials, TV shows, and films—and outside their small field, they're fairly anonymous. My neighbor's name is Chuck and he's been working with his partner Lenny for fifteen years. They're an odd Mutt and Jeff pairing. Chuck is a big, noisy, outsized personality, while Lenny is more of the cautious, quiet scholar. Chuck is the showman, while Lenny is the idea man who handles their business dealings. They're both solid musicians and wordsmiths, but when they pitch their material, Chuck dominates the show, while Lenny is content to sit in the background, piping up only when needed. They're friends professionally, but even though they live twenty minutes from each other in Southern California, they don't socialize. In fifteen years, they've never had dinner together with their wives. And yet they work seamlessly together, bouncing ideas for hooks and lyrics back and forth, never arguing about who wrote what or who deserves credit for their latest success.

It was a perfect partnership, the classic example of one plus one equaling three—until they got into a spat over a business deal. The details are too trivial to repeat here, but the net result was that Chuck felt that Lenny had not fully taken Chuck's interests into consideration on a deal. And he was angry about it.

Suddenly the two partners were trading angry phone calls and e-mails, which escalated into a nastiness so pungent that Lenny actually showed me some of the cruel zingers he had written to Chuck (I guess he was proud of his witty ripostes).

"This is childish," I said.

"Well, he's wrong," said Lenny. "I'm not trying to cheat him."

"I'm sure that's true," I said, "but ratcheting up the insults isn't going to change his mind. Something else is going on here, and you're going to bust up a great partnership if you don't figure it out."

A day later Lenny called me.

"I've got it," he said. "As long as I've known Chuck, he's always picking fights. He has at least one a day, because he loves talking about it. If someone is chewing popcorn too loudly behind him at the movies, he'll pick a fight. He'll complain if the maître d' shows him to an inferior table at a restaurant or if a dish is lukewarm. He's the kind of guy who sends back wine. He argues with plumbers and electricians over their bills. He argues with New York cabdrivers for not taking the best route. He thinks people who don't return his phone calls right away are disrespecting him. In fact, everything that happens to Chuck is a test of whether he's being respected or dismissed. That's how he sees the world.

"That's when it hit me: Chuck's whole life is a series of incidents where he takes umbrage at some perceived offense. He's a Serial Umbrage Taker."

By naming it, Lenny had zeroed in on the problem—and framed it in a humorous way that made Chuck's behavior palatable. But it wasn't of much use if he couldn't share this insight to patch things up with his partner.

The same day, Lenny called Chuck and told him the sniping had to stop. Then he took a deep breath and offered Chuck his "analysis" of his personality.

"I've got a name for why you're like this," said Lenny. "You're a Serial Umbrage Taker. You live to take umbrage."

The other end of the line went dead for a few interminable seconds.

Finally, Chuck started laughing hysterically and responded. "I have to call my wife. She'll love this. You've just nailed me."

And with that simple naming gesture, their fight was over. Lenny had not only gained an insight into Chuck's behavior, he had a name for it that Chuck both accepted and reveled in. Chuck now signs all his e-mails to his partner with "Umbrage."

What's in a name? More than we know.

Tool #14:
Give Your Friends a Lifetime Pass

I have a friend named Phillip who helped me out in a significant way. His recommendations have led to me working with three of my favorite clients. I am still great friends with these clients, and (I am sure) my relationship with them has helped me meet other wonderful people. I owe a lot to Phillip. Take him out of the equation and these relationships never would have happened. That's what makes Phillip one of at least fifty people in my life to whom, at least once a year, I say thank you for making my life better.

Phillip's an interesting fellow. He's brilliant, creative, personable, but a bit of an unmade bed when it comes to fulfilling small commitments. His ideas are so good that they sometimes pay off in a big way, which is why he's successful. But he balances out all that good with minor screw-ups that can be incredibly annoying. Over the years he has disappointed me in a number of little ways, things like last-minute cancellations. They're petty annoyances that add a little disturbance to my life, not violent earthquakes that will sunder our relationship.

Phillip is always contrite and apologetic about these things. And I always accept his apology with the same words. I tell him, "Phillip, when I weigh all the good things you have done for me against the times you've let me down, you are so far ahead on good stuff that you have a lifetime pass." It makes him feel good. It makes me feel even better (forgiving someone will do that for you). And we remain friends.

You could make the argument that I'm "enabling" Phillip's screwup behavior by excusing it. But that's not what's going on here. To me it's a matter of perspective. When I consider Phillip's actions, I ask myself one question: Am I better off or worse off because of having this person in my life? (I call this the Ronald Reagan Question, because he won the presidency in 1980 by asking voters, "Are you better off now than you were four years ago?" and then won again in 1984 by asking the same question.) With Phillip, the answer will always be in his favor. Phillip has done such wonderful things for me—and I am so grateful—that they will forever override any conceivable negative behavior. That's the power of a lifetime pass.

Now let me ask you: How many people in your life have you given a lifetime pass? A more probing question: Do you think the number is too high or too low?

My hunch is that, for most people, we believe that our number should be higher! It's a hunch based on all the times people have regaled me with stories of ruptured friendships caused by someone else's "unforgivable" behavior. We've all heard these stories. We've all had it happen to us. It's quite possible that we've committed the atrocious behavior ourselves and lost a friend in the process.

It's a fairly common drama of modern life. I had dinner once with my friend Edward, who is a successful management consultant. I brought up the name of a mutual acquaintance, also in the field, with whom Edward often did business. Edward stopped me and, waving his dinner fork like a sword, said, "I don't talk about him anymore. He's dead to me."

A statement like that is too intriguing to let go, so I pressed Edward for details. What horror could this fellow have perpetrated that could sunder a long and mutually profitable relationship? Edward overcame his professed reluctance to talk about the man and spun for me a tale that I expected to end with an act of heinous perfidy. In the end, the unforgivable act was a lapse in phone-call etiquette. The former friend had neglected to inform Edward about a meeting with someone they were dealing with together. It wasn't a criminal act. It wasn't unethical. It probably wasn't intentional, just one of those communication lapses that happen in people's busy schedules. But Edward, for whatever reason, saw it as unpardonable sneakiness.

That's it? I thought. An overlooked phone call?

It made me wonder. What if Edward, instead of fuming about a perceived (and possibly misinterpreted) slight, had asked himself the Ronald Reagan Question: Is my life better off or worse off because this fellow is in it? If he had done that, they would still be friends. And you always want to be growing the number of friends in your life, not shrinking it.

The odd thing is that we already do this—with our families. Who among us, after all, hasn't endured some hurtful remark or interpersonal abuse by a sibling, a son or daughter, a mother or father? And yet we accept and forgive these slights and misdemeanors because they involve a blood relation. Members of our family get a lifetime pass.

That's the tool of acceptance that I'm recommending here. If we can be that forgiving with family members, why can't we extend the same level of acceptance to people who, when all is said and done, have demonstrably made our lives better? All we have to do is ask the Ronald Reagan Question—and accept the answer.

This is not just an exercise in gratitude. It forces us to confront the humbling fact that we have not achieved our success on our own. We had help along the way. In that sense, the lifetime pass does double duty. It not only reminds us to keep our friends close (even when they sometimes let us down), but it also provides a perspective that we often forget, the one where we see that we're not alone.

To maintain great Mojo, make a list of all of the people who have significantly helped you have a great life. Let them know that your life is better off because you have known them. Give them a "lifetime pass"! Who knows? Maybe they will even give you a "lifetime pass" in return.

Connecting
Inside to Outside

CHAPTER 16

Going Beyond Self-Help

There's no getting around it: This is a self-help book. Everything you've read in this book's first three sections is about improving something about *yourself*. When we've discussed the facets of identity, achievement, reputation, and acceptance that affect Mojo, the focus has always been on shaping a happier, more confident, more engaged *you*.

But there's something we haven't brought up yet and it may be the most critical piece of advice within these pages: *You should not feel obligated to do any of this alone!* If you want to improve your performance at almost anything, your odds of success improve considerably the moment you enlist someone else to help you.

I know this from personal experience, because for the past few years I have enlisted the help of a friend, Jim Moore, in achieving my own personal goals. Every day, no matter where either of us is in the world, we try to connect on the phone so Jim can ask me a series of questions. They're important day-to-day lifestyle questions such as "Did you say or do anything nice for Lyda [my wife]?"; "How much do you weigh?"; or "How many minutes did you write?" Jim happens to be an esteemed expert in leadership development, but his qualifications for this ritual rest more on the fact that he's a friend who's genuinely interested in helping me and will always make himself available for our daily phone call.

The process is incredibly simple. At the end of each day, Jim asks me seventeen questions (the number has changed over time as my goals shift between maintaining my weight and being nicer to my family). Each question has to be answered with a yes, no, or a number. I record the results on an Excel spreadsheet and at the end of the week get an assessment of how well I'm sticking to my objectives. (I return the favor by asking Jim a series of seventeen questions about what matters to him.)

The results are astonishing. After the first eighteen months of adhering to this ritual, Jim and I both weighed exactly what we wanted to weigh, exercised more, and got more done (and I was nicer to my wife). As an experiment, we quit for about a year to see what would happen. Each of us put the weight back on and did not achieve nearly as much—a result that was both predictable, depressing, and sent us rushing back to the program, where we resumed hitting our targets immediately. I was never unhappy, but my life seems happier and more meaningful to me when I use this process.

(To see my "daily questions," Jim's daily questions, and get an article describing this process, go to www.MojoTheBook.com.)

The lesson is clear: We don't just have to rely on self-help!

Some of us already practice this instinctively, when we enlist a friend to attend yoga class with us or commit to training for a marathon (an inherently lonely sport) the moment a friend agrees to join us. We enjoy the companionship and support, but knowing we're answerable to someone else, even if it's only to schedule a time for a training run, is also motivating. That small obligation keeps us focused. The longer we stick with it and the nearer we get to the finish line, the closer the bond between the two of us. At some point we reach a point of no return where we don't want to disappoint a friend or don't want to be the first to give up (we're competitive that way, and that's good). Pairing up provides us with a discipline that we cannot summon as readily working solo.

This "power of two" thinking works well for overt personal objectives such as quitting smoking or losing weight or athletic training, where we're relying more on moral support (a friend likened it to "training wheels"), rather than instructive coaching, to reach a clearly marked finish line.

But enlisting someone else to help us isn't our first impulse when we dive into a self-improvement campaign involving our professional lives. Whether it's upgrading the quality of our customer base, or landing a big promotion, or executing a career U-turn, our initial impulse is to do it on our own. After all, it's our goal, our effort, our accomplishment, and our payoff if we succeed. How can we share the burden—and glory—with someone else?

Part of the reason behind this is psychic self-preservation on our part; if we fall short of our goal, we want to contain the failure to a circle of one: ourselves. If no one knows what we're striving for, then no one can criticize us for faltering.

But the far bigger reason is that puckish mental blocker known as ego. It's the reason some people (more often men) can't ask for directions when they're lost. We can't admit that we need help. We can't accept that someone else might know more than we do about how we can change for the better. We believe any achievement of ours is somehow diminished if we don't do it entirely by ourselves. If there's credit to be had, we want it all to ourselves.

I recall a few years back when I happened to be sitting on the sidelines watching two women I knew well compete for the same editor-in-chief job at a magazine. The interview process was rigorous—and eventually turned into a "bake-off" where both of the women had to submit their ideas for two complete issues of the magazine. Coming up with stories and headlines for two issues was a lot of work. But what intrigued me was the two women's different approaches to the same challenge. Lily was a bold, self-confident editor who was accustomed to being the star in any setting—i.e., she had a healthy ego and it was a vital part of her skill set. Upon getting instructions for the "bake-off," Lily left her office, waved good-bye to her husband and kids, and secreted herself in a friend's week-end home, where she put together the two issues all by herself in three days. She handed her entry in ahead of the deadline, proud that it was her best work.

Lily's rival for the job was Sarah. If Lily was the nimble hare, Sarah was a plodding turtle. She was no less confident in her creative abilities than Lily, but she didn't wear her ego on her sleeve. She approached the challenge as an exercise in collegial thinking rather than as a star turn. She called up a dozen trusted friends, asking for story ideas, clever head-lines, and the names of possible contributors. Then she assembled the suggestions in a laundry list and started doing what she was trained for: editing. She tossed out what she didn't like and kept what appealed to her.

Observing this process, I couldn't have asked for a starker contrast between the merits of going it alone or seeking the help of others. Lily wanted to do it all by herself. She wanted to write up her plans, put them in a beautiful box, wrap it up with a pink ribbon, and present it to the judges as if it were a gift and she expected a gold star for her efforts. Sarah had her eye on a different prize, knowing that the only thing that mattered was the end product, not whether the ideas had originated with her or someone else. That inclusive approach delivered more good ideas. Sarah got the job.*

That's the approach—Sarah's, not Lily's—that I want you to assume as you tackle the goal of building or recapturing your Mojo. Don't let your ego block you from your goals. Start seeing every challenge as a choice between (a) *I can do it by myself* and (b) *I may be able to do it better with help.*

Once you accept that you are judged more on the result than on how many hands played a part in achieving it, you'll make the right choice.

---

* When you think about it, most organizations are set up to encourage us to seek help when we need it. That's the entire assumption behind the collective entity known as "the corporation": Some tasks are better achieved by groups than by individuals. The only puzzling part is: Why do we fight what's built into the "system"?

Coda:
You Go First

"When my children grow up, I want them to be . . ."

I have asked thousands of parents from around the world to give me *one word* to complete this sentence.

No matter what country I am in, one word is spoken more than every other word combined.

What is that one word?

Happy!

Do you want your children to be happy? Do you want your parents to be happy? Do you want the people who love you at home to be happy? Do you want the people who respect you at work to be happy?

You go first.

You be happy.

The people who love you want you to be happy.

Mojo is—that positive spirit—toward what you are doing—that starts from the inside—and radiates to the outside.

Do you want the people that you love and respect to have Mojo?

Show them yours!

There are good people out there who look up to us. They respect us. They want to be like us. We are role models for them.

What message do we send to the people we love at home when we communicate that we are unhappy and that our lives at home are meaningless?

Being with you does not bring me joy and my life at home really doesn't matter that much to me.

What message do we send to the people who we respect at work when we communicate that we are unhappy and that our jobs are meaningless?

I wish I were not here today. I would rather be doing almost anything than working with you or in this company.

On the other hand, what message do we send to the people—at work and home—when our Mojo is high?

I find joy in my life when I am with you. Being with you—in this home or in this workplace—matters to me. You are important and what I am doing with you is important.

Is there any better message that we can communicate to the people who trust us, respect us, and love us?

I can't think of one.

My goal in writing this book is, in some small way, to try to help you have a happier and more meaningful life. By doing this, you will help the wonderful people in your life find more happiness and meaning.

Don't just do it for you.

Do it for them!

Appendix I

The Mojo Survey: Measuring Short-Term Satisfaction (Happiness) and Long-Term Benefit (Meaning)

(To complete the Mojo Survey online, please go to www.MojoTheBook.com. You can then see how your answers compare with the results from thousands of respondents who have completed the survey.)

For this study, we would like you to think about the time that you spend both at work and outside of work.

We would like you to consider your time in two dimensions: short-term satisfaction (or happiness) and long-term benefit (or meaning).

Short-term satisfaction (happiness) can be defined as satisfaction with the activity itself. For example, questions like "Does this activity make me happy?" or "Do I find gratification in the activity itself?" can help us gauge the degree of short-term satisfaction that we gain from any activity.

Long-term benefit (meaning) can be defined as the positive outcomes that result from engaging in the activity. Questions like "Are the results achieved from this activity worth my effort?" or "Is the successful completion of this activity going to have a long-term positive impact on my life?" can help us gauge our expectations for the potential long-term benefit from any activity.

The figure on the next page illustrates five different combinations of short-term satisfaction and long-term benefit that can characterize our relationship to any activity—either at work or outside of work.

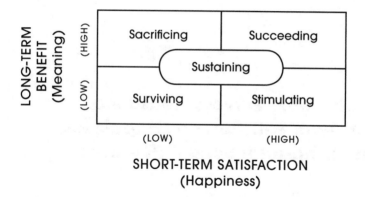

SHORT-TERM SATISFACTION
(Happiness)

We would like you to read a description of each potential combination of short-term satisfaction and long-term benefit, then answer a few questions.

Stimulating is a term for activities that score high in short-term satisfaction but low in long-term benefit. An example of a stimulating activity might be watching sitcoms on TV. Watching sitcoms may not do much harm, and for some people may be a fun way to pass time, but on the other hand, time spent watching sitcoms will not lead to long-term achievement. At work, gossiping with coworkers may be fun for a while, but it is probably not career- or business-enhancing. A life spent solely on stimulating activities could provide a lot of short-term pleasure but little long-term achievement.

Please list some examples of activities you find *stimulating* (high short-term satisfaction, low long-term benefit)?

_____

_____

At work, what percent of your time is spent engaging in *stimulating* activities?

_____ (maximum = 100%)

Outside of work, what percent of your time is spent engaging in *stimulating* activities?

_____ (maximum = 100%)

Sacrificing is a term for activities that score low in short-term satisfaction but high in long-term benefit. An extreme example of sacrificing could involve dedicating your life to work that you hate because you feel like you "have to" to achieve a larger goal. A more common example might be working out when you don't feel like it in order to improve your long-term health. At work, sacrificing might be spending extra hours on that report (when you could have gone to the ball game) to help enhance your career prospects. A life spent solely on sacrificing activities would be the life of a martyr—lots of achievement, but not much joy.

Please list some examples of activities you engage in where you feel you are *sacrificing* (low short-term satisfaction, high long-term benefit)?

_____

_____

At work, what percent of your time is spent engaging in activities where you feel you are *sacrificing*?

_____ (maximum = 100%)

Outside of work, what percent of your time is spent engaging in activities where you feel you are sacrificing?

_____ (maximum = 100%)

Surviving is a term for activities that score low on short-term satisfaction and low on long-term benefit. These are activities that don't cause much joy or satisfaction and do not contribute to long-term benefit in your life. These are typically activities that we are doing because we feel that we have to do them in order to just "get by." Charles Dickens frequently described the lives of people who were almost constantly in the surviving box. These poor people had countless hours of hard work, not much joy, and not much to show for all of their efforts. A life spent solely on surviving activities would be a hard life indeed.

Please list some examples of activities you engage in where you feel you are *surviving* (low short-term satisfaction, low long-term benefit)?

_____

_____

At work, what percent of your time is spent engaging in activities where you feel you are *surviving*?

_____ (maximum = 100%)

Outside of work, what percent of your time is spent engaging in activities where you feel you are *surviving*?

_____ (maximum = 100%)

Sustaining is a term for activities that produce moderate amounts of short-term satisfaction and lead to moderate long-term benefits. For many professionals, the daily answering of e-mails is a sustaining activity—it is moderately interesting (not thrilling) and usually produces moderate long-term benefit (not life-changing). At home, some might consider the day-to-day routines of shopping, cooking, and cleaning to be in the sustaining category. A life spent solely on sustaining activities would be an okay life—not great, yet not too bad.

Please list some examples of activities you engage in where you feel you are *sustaining* (moderate short-term satisfaction, moderate long-term benefit)?

_____

_____

At work, what percent of your time is spent engaging in activities where you feel you are *sustaining*?

_____ (maximum = 100%)

Outside of work, what percent of your time is spent engaging in activities where you feel you are *sustaining*?

_____ (maximum = 100%)

Succeeding is a term for activities that score high on short-term satisfaction and high on long-term benefit. These activities are the ones that we love to do—and get great benefit from doing. At work, people who spend a lot of time in the succeeding box love what they are doing and believe that it is producing long-term benefit at the same time. At home, a parent may be spending hours with a child—time that the parent greatly enjoys, while valuing the long-term benefit that will come to the child. A life spent in succeeding is a life that is filled with both joy and accomplishment.

Please list some examples of activities you engage in where you feel you are *succeeding* (high short-term satisfaction, high long-term benefit)?

_____

_____

At work, what percent of your time is spent engaging in activities where you feel you are *succeeding*?

_____ (maximum = 100%)

Outside of work, what percent of your time is spent engaging in activities where you feel you are *succeeding*?

_____ (maximum = 100%)

Now we would like you to please consider *all* of the time that you spend *at work* in a *normal* workweek.

Please report what percent of your time spent *at work* falls into each of the five categories below.

Please do NOT include a percent sign in your response. (Note: The percentages should total 100.)

	PERCENT OF TIME SPENT
Stimulating (high short-term satisfaction, low long-term benefit)	
Sacrificing (low short-term satisfaction, high long-term benefit)	

continued	PERCENT OF TIME SPENT
Surviving (low short-term satisfaction, low long-term benefit)	
Sustaining (moderate short-term satisfaction, moderate long-term benefit)	
Succeeding (high short-term satisfaction, high long-term benefit)	

Now we would like you to please consider *all* of the time that you spend *outside of work* in a *normal* week.

Please report what percent of your time spent *outside of work* falls into each of the five categories below.

Please do NOT include a percent sign in your response. (Note: The percentages should total 100.)

	PERCENT OF TIME SPENT
Stimulating (high short-term satisfaction, low long-term benefit)	
Sacrificing (low short-term satisfaction, high long-term benefit)	
Surviving (low short-term satisfaction, low long-term benefit)	
Sustaining (moderate short-term satisfaction, moderate long-term benefit)	
Succeeding (high short-term satisfaction, high long-term benefit)	

Now we would like you to think about people you work with or know.

Please consider *all* of the time that the *average employed adult* spends *at work* in a *normal* workweek.

Please give us your best estimate of what percent of their time spent *at work* falls into each of the five categories below.

Please do NOT include a percent sign in your response. (Note: The percentages should total 100.)

	PERCENT OF TIME SPENT
Stimulating (high short-term satisfaction, low long-term benefit)	
Sacrificing (low short-term satisfaction, high long-term benefit)	
Surviving (low short-term satisfaction, low long-term benefit)	
Sustaining (moderate short-term satisfaction, moderate long-term benefit)	
Succeeding (high short-term satisfaction, high long-term benefit)	

Now please consider *all* of the time that the *average employed adult* spends *outside of work* in a *normal* week.

Please give us your best estimate of what percent of their time spent *outside of work* falls into each of the five categories below.

Please do NOT include a percent sign in your response. (Note: The percentages should total 100.)

	PERCENT OF TIME SPENT
Stimulating (high short-term satisfaction, low long-term benefit)	
Sacrificing (low short-term satisfaction, high long-term benefit)	
Surviving (low short-term satisfaction, low long-term benefit)	

continued	PERCENT OF TIME SPENT
Sustaining (moderate short-term satisfaction, moderate long-term benefit)	
Succeeding (high short-term satisfaction, high long-term benefit)	

Now please describe how satisfied *you* are *overall* with both your work life and your life outside of work:

Work life
○ Very Dissatisfied
○ Dissatisfied
○ Somewhat Dissatisfied
○ Neutral
○ Somewhat Satisfied
○ Satisfied
○ Very Satisfied

Life outside of work
○ Very Dissatisfied
○ Dissatisfied
○ Somewhat Dissatisfied
○ Neutral
○ Somewhat Satisfied
○ Satisfied
○ Very Satisfied

Finally, we have a few additional questions about your background. These will be used to help us interpret the data.

What is your gender?
○ Male
○ Female

What is your level of education?

◯ High school
◯ Some college
◯ College degree
◯ Some graduate school
◯ Graduate degree

How would you classify your occupation?

◯ Non-manager
◯ Manager
◯ Executive
◯ Self-employed and/or entrepreneur
◯ Other
◯ Retired

How many years have you been working in your current job or a very similar job within the same industry? _____

On an *average weekday,* how many hours do you spend doing the following activities?

Your answer can be a portion of an hour, for example, for 30 minutes you would enter 0.5. (Note: The total number of hours should not exceed 24.)

	NUMBER OF HOURS
Working (including working from home, for example, answering e-mails)	
Commuting to and from work	
Physical fitness	
Spending quality time at home with family or loved ones	
Socializing out of the home (dining out, movies, theater, museums, sports games)	
Watching television (sitcoms, news, sports)	

continued	NUMBER OF HOURS
Reading for non-work (for example, books, magazines, etc.)	
Using the Internet or computer for non-work activities (for example, surfing the Internet, social networking, YouTube, etc.)	
Household chores (laundry, dishes, maintenance)	

What is your marital status?
○ Single
○ Married
○ Divorced
○ Widowed

What is your age?
○ Under 21
○ 21–29
○ 30–39
○ 40–49
○ 50–59
○ 60 and over

How many children do you have? _____

Appendix II

What the Mojo
Survey Results Mean

The Mojo Survey is primarily a self-assessment inventory designed to give respondents the opportunity to evaluate how they spend their time and what percentage of their time produces short-term satisfaction (happiness) and/or long-term benefit (meaning)—both at work and outside of work. The survey also gives respondents the opportunity to estimate the experience of short-term satisfaction and long-term benefit for the "average" employee in the "average" corporation.

If you would like to have your results included in this ongoing study, please go to www.MojoTheBook.com. Click on the Mojo Survey button on the home page. After completing the survey, you will be able to see how your scores compare to the scores of thousands of other respondents. You may wish to complete the survey now—before you turn to the next page—so that your answers will not be biased by what you learn about the results from others.

At the time of this writing, more than three thousand respondents have already completed the Mojo Survey. This group is clearly not representative of all human beings or employees in general, but may well be representative of my readers. Almost all of the respondents are in professional, managerial, or entrepreneurial roles. Almost all are college graduates and more than half have graduate degrees. If you are reading this book, you probably are (or have been) a professional, manager, or entrepreneur—or have aspirations to become one.

The "Average" Employee

When respondents were asked how they thought "average" employees in an "average" company were spending their time (both at work and outside of work), the following patterns emerged:

AT WORK:

Surviving: 24.2%
Stimulating: 19.1%
Sacrificing: 17.0%
Sustaining: 23.4%
Succeeding: 16.3%

OUTSIDE OF WORK:

Surviving: 19.2%
Stimulating: 29.4%
Sacrificing: 14.4%
Sustaining: 20.8%
Succeeding: 15.6%

When I asked a panel of forty "experts"* in the field to provide their estimates on the "average" employee, the results were almost identical to our respondent scores.

The results of our survey (not surprisingly) show that the major difference between work and home for the "average" employees is that more time is spent in *stimulating* activities outside of work—and correspondingly less time in the other categories.

The Professional, Manager, and Entrepreneur

When the respondents in the database were asked to describe how they spent their *own* time, a significantly different pattern emerged:

AT WORK:

Surviving: 14.4%
Stimulating: 15.2%
Sacrificing: 17.8%
Sustaining: 22.7%
Succeeding: 29.9%

OUTSIDE OF WORK:

Surviving: 11.4%
Stimulating: 21.2%
Sacrificing: 15.4%
Sustaining: 21.9%
Succeeding: 30.1%

---

* These experts were either widely recognized authors in the field, chief learning officers, or chief human resources officers in major corporations.

Looking at the self-assessments of the survey, raters reported that they spent a substantially greater percentage of their time *succeeding* than the "average" employee, both at work and at home. This is not surprising for two reasons: (1) this group of raters (in terms of socioeconomic achievement) *was* far more successful than an "average" sample of employees (for example, more than 50 percent of those surveyed had a graduate degree), and (2) all people tend to overrate themselves relative to their professional peers (even if their peers are doing as well as they are).

The self-assessments of the survey takers were substantially lower on *stimulating* activities (especially at home). This is not surprising for two reasons: (1) people higher in socioeconomic achievement *may actually* spend more time outside of work in developmental or learning activities (as opposed to watching TV), and (2) people higher in socioeconomic achievement clearly *believe* that "average" people spend more time in the *stimulating* category than they do.

Correlations Between All Categories at Work and at Home

One of the most interesting findings of our research to date—*the way that we experience our time at work versus how we experience time at home*—is highly correlated in every category.

> Surviving at work—surviving outside of work+.483*
> Stimulating at work—stimulating outside of work+.442*
> Sacrificing at work—sacrificing outside of work+.295*
> Sustaining at work—sustaining at home+.560*
> Succeeding at work—succeeding outside of work+.581*

> * denotes statistical significance, $p < 0.001$

These findings paint a clear picture. Our *activities* at work and outside of work are clearly different. Yet our *experience* of both short-term satisfaction and long-term benefit at work and outside of work are highly correlated. What does this mean?

Our experience of happiness and meaning in life is influenced by who we are—as much as by what we are doing.

The implications of this research are simple, yet profound. If you want to experience more happiness and meaning in your relationship to any activity, you have two simple choices: (1) change the activity, or (2) change yourself. If you cannot change the activity, option one is eliminated. But, as our research indicates, the activity is only a part of your experience of happiness and meaning. In many cases *we* are more responsible for the experience of happiness and meaning in life than whatever we are doing.

What Does Each Category Mean to You?

Survey participants were asked to name specific activities that fit each category for them. Some of the most common themes were:

Surviving: doing "chores," cleaning, paying bills, paying taxes, dealing with people that you feel you *have to* but don't *want to,* boring meetings at work, waiting, "administrative detail," and commuting.

Stimulating: watching TV, surfing the net for fun, watching sports, playing video games, reading "junk" fiction, relationship-free sex, gossiping with coworkers, flirting, bashing upper management, and brainstorming at work that is interesting but that we know will amount to nothing.

Sacrificing: "watching TV (that I don't like) with my partner," "spending time with people I don't like," eating "healthy" foods that taste bland, getting organized, cleaning up the office, "making sure I am 'politically correct,'" documentation, working late and on weekends, and "doing work that I can't stand but need to do to 'get ahead.'"

Sustaining: taking my family to the mall, attending home owners meetings, "check-in" e-mails, managing projects, reading that is required to keep up, traveling for business, regular follow-up with clients, "update" meetings, routine communication, and "doing the 'medium impact' parts of my job."

Succeeding: "spending time with people I love," "spending time with my grandchildren" (an amazing number of specific comments on this), "reading books that are meaningful for me," "listening to helpful audios while I am commuting," satisfying client work, teaching and developing other people, and successfully completing important projects.

Some activities tended to cluster around certain categories. For example, anything called a "chore" tended to go in *surviving*, watching sports went in *stimulating*, eating healthy yet tasteless foods went in *sacrificing*, routing communication, i.e., e-mailing, tended to go in *sustaining*, and meaningful project completion was almost always in *succeeding*.

On the other hand, in several cases the exact same activity was placed by different people in every category. For example, exercising, gardening, going to grad school, and coaching employees were all mentioned at least once in every category. This diversity of responses reinforces the point that in some cases our lower Mojo scores are a function of the activity, but in many cases they are a function of our unique attitude toward the activity.

Overall Satisfaction at Work and Home

Along with specific questions about how they were spending their time, respondents were asked to rate their overall satisfaction both at work and outside work. As it turns out there was a positive correlation between satisfaction with work and satisfaction outside work (+.336 *). In other words respondents who were satisfied with their home life tended to be the same respondents who were satisfied with their work life.

When the five Mojo categories were compared to overall satisfaction at work, not surprisingly, spending more time in the *succeeding* category was highly positively correlated with overall work satisfaction and spending time in the *surviving* category was highly negatively correlated with overall work satisfaction. The same correlations appeared when *surviving* and *succeeding* were compared to overall satisfaction outside work.

Perhaps more interesting was the fact that time spent in *stimulating* or *sacrificing* was negatively correlated with overall satisfaction both at work and outside of work. What these results indicate is that neither experiencing happiness without meaning or experiencing meaning without happiness lead to greater overall satisfaction at work or at home. The percent of time spent in the *sustaining* category was seen as not significantly correlated with overall satisfaction—either at work or at home.

Our biggest surprise in analyzing these results was the slightly negative correlation between the time spent on *stimulating* activities at home and overall satisfaction with home life. Before reviewing the results, I assumed that, for most people, "outside work" was a place to just have fun. In hindsight, I realize I was wrong. There is absolutely no evidence that increased time spent on watching TV, surfing the net, or playing video games increases overall satisfaction with life outside of work.

The implications of our findings are clear: To increase your overall satisfaction at work and outside work you need to increase the percent of time that you are spending on activities that are providing *both* short-term satisfaction and long-term benefit at the same time. You need to decrease the amount of time that you are spending on activities that fall under the headings *surviving, sacrificing,* and *stimulating.* Since the categories "work" and "outside work" cover our entire lives (with the exception of sleep), it seems clear that the only way to increase your overall satisfaction with life is to focus on activities that provide both meaning and happiness.

Correlation with overall work satisfaction
Surviving −.460*
Stimulating −.088*
Sacrificing −.244*
Sustaining − +.001
Succeeding +.508*

Correlation with overall satisfaction outside work
Surviving −.348*
Stimulating −.122*
Sacrificing −.152*
Sustaining −.046
Succeeding +.385*

Index